137

TEACHING OUR FAITH IN GOD

TEACHING
OUR FAITH
IN GOD

L. Harold DeWolf

ABINGDON PRESS NEW YORK   NASHVILLE

TEACHING OUR FAITH IN GOD

Copyright © 1963 by Abingdon Press

Library of Congress Catalog Card Number: 63-7480

SET UP, PRINTED, AND BOUND BY THE
PARTHENON PRESS, AT NASHVILLE,
TENNESSEE, UNITED STATES OF AMERICA

Acknowledgments

FROM 1958 TO 1960 I WAS PRIVILEGED TO SERVE AS THEOLOGICAL consultant to the Curriculum Study Committee in the Division of Christian Education, National Council of the Churches of Christ in the U.S.A. Those were very important years in which we worked out policies now providing the basis for curriculum preparation in many churches of the United States and Canada. I am deeply grateful to the able staff and members of the Curriculum Study Committee for the many courtesies shown to me and for all I learned from these representatives of nearly all sizable Protestant churches in North America. Participants in the work of those years will recognize in this book my personal responses to many issues discussed in the meetings of the committee. Dr. D. Campbell Wyckoff especially stimulated my thinking. Chapters Two and Three include much material which I first prepared for papers presented to the Curriculum Committee.

Chapters Four through Seven are based on lectures presented at the University of the Pacific as the Colliver Lectures of 1960. Chapters Eight through Eleven are revisions of the Mendenhall Lectures which I gave at DePauw University in 1961 before the pastors of the Indiana Council of Churches. To the presidents, faculty members, and staff personnel of those two universities who treated me so generously I make grateful acknowledgment.

My thoughts on Christian education have been further instructed and stimulated in formal and informal consultation with the Curriculum Committee and staff members of the

Board of Education of The Methodist Church. Some members of the Methodist staff have also generously prepared critical notes on the manuscript of this book.

My colleagues in Boston University School of Theology, who are specialists in religious education, have all made important contributions to my thought. With Professors Walter L. Holcomb and William Clifton Moore I have had many instructive conversations on various relevant issues. Professor Donald M. Maynard has been of similar assistance. In addition, he has brought me into one of his graduate seminars for critical discussion and has given the manuscript of this book a painstaking, critical reading. Of course he and my other friendly critics are not responsible for the point of view or the shortcomings of this book, but I am indebted to them for many improvements in it.

There is no way to learn equal to teaching. I am grateful to the many hundreds of students who have taught me, their teacher, in church schools of Nebraska, Massachusetts, and Southern Rhodesia; in pastors' schools, lay institutes, colleges and theological schools of the United States and several African countries; and especially in my classes at Boston University.

Finally, I acknowledge with warm gratitude the indispensable aid of my wife. Not only did she carefully type the manuscript of this book, like each of its seven predecessors from my pen, but in the rearing of our children she has taught me much about Christian nurture.

L. HAROLD DEWOLF

Contents

Introduction

CHRISTIAN EDUCATION IS A WORK OF TEACHING.[1] THE SAME NAME is used for the study of that work.

The study of the Christian message taught by Christian educators is called theology.

The study of the message and the study of the work of teaching the message belong together. Theology and Christian education need each other.

Theology needs religious education[2] for two principal reasons. First, religious education should be of great help in clarifying the language of theology for real communication. Many theologians are notoriously obscure. The business of theology is such interpretation of our Christian faith as may enable us to communicate it to the contemporary world. If this interpretation is successful, it should lead to clarity and persuasiveness. Unfortunately, theologians often talk mainly to each other. In this kind of introverted communication there frequently develops a peculiar language understood by few excepting theologians. Indeed, a poorly kept trade secret is that often theologians do not even understand each other. Such writing is often stimulating to the mind as a mental exercise and may even be highly suggestive to especially trained readers. However, it fails to accomplish the more important purposes of theology.

[1] The word "teaching," here and elsewhere, is used in its broadest sense. It will be emphasized later that this includes much else besides formal instruction by a teacher in front of a class.

[2] In this book the phrases "Christian education" and "religious education" are used interchangeably.

Religious educators are in communication with people of all ages within the church itself and, indeed, with many who are in only a marginal relation to the church. In the face-to-face relations common in Christian education, it often becomes embarrassingly evident to the teacher that communication is not successfully taking place. When the language that has been used has been provided by theologians, there needs to be a feedback from religious education to theology letting theologians know that what they have intended to be the language of communication is not actually communicating. Without such feedbacks, theology threatens to become an esoteric conversation in a corner while the church and the world go by. This is an exercise in futility.

Moreover, it is through religious education that the doctrine concerning our Christian faith, so carefully interpreted and elaborated by theologians, may actually become taught in the world. If the limitations of the analogy can be accepted, we may say that theology needs Christian education as seriously as the manufacturer needs the retail merchant. The products of theological labor were not intended to gather dust in storage on the shelves of theologians.

On the other hand, religious education sorely needs theology. Some writers and many teachers in the field of Christian education have gained their understanding of the Christian faith from sources that have not plumbed to the depth of the Christian message. Sometimes the Christian educator has drawn the message from past statements of theological interpretation now scarcely relevant to present culture and life. This has happened especially frequently during a period in which there has occurred a radical estrangement between theology and religious education. People who are teaching the Christian faith need to be teaching it in the worthiest forms in which it has been interpreted for their own age. This implies the necessity of genuine conversation between theology and religious education.

Moreover, many problems of pedagogical method are profoundly theological. Method is determined by the ideas we hold of what a child is, what constitutes spiritual growth, what the goal toward which we are working is, and who the participants in the work of Christian education are. Every one of these issues is theological to the very core; that is, the Christian message has much to say about these selfsame matters. Religious education, therefore, needs conversations with theology in order to learn certain critical statements of Christian first principles which have important implications for method as well as for the determination of goal and message.

It is a special pleasure for me personally to be involved in this effort to join more closely the two disciplines. Ever since, as a high school senior, I began to teach a Sunday School class and also began to study my father's theological books, I have been engaged in both disciplines. In order that the reader may know how far I am from having a detached, merely speculative interest in religious education, I will indulge in some further personal references here. During the last forty-three years I have served almost continuously as a volunteer teacher in Sunday school, moving, according to local needs, up and down through the age scale from the junior department to the adults, down again to the kindergarten and back to the adults. I have recently completed five years of continuous teaching in a high school class which is my pride and delight.

Pedagogical difficulties have always especially intrigued me. Few problems have ever fascinated me more than those confronted in teaching, in the same years, the meaning of the same Christian faith to doctoral candidates in the university and to kindergartners in the Sunday school; or, in Rhodesia writing for theological journals in America while regularly teaching in a theological school for African pastors and, as a volunteer, in a class of African high school boys. If there is any work more fascinating, more sacred, or more rewarding to the worker than Christian religious education, I have not found it.

I am grateful for the two years served recently as theological consultant to the Curriculum Study Committee in the Division of Christian Education, National Council of the Churches of

Christ in the U.S.A. and for similar associations with the Curriculum Committee of The Methodist Board of Education. These associations with some of the best professional Christian educators, in intensive shop talk, have been immensely stimulating to me.

At the same time I must confess to serious limitations for this work. I am not a specialist in the teaching of children, nor of young people, nor of adults in the local church, though I am an experienced amateur. Many specialists have read much more widely and carefully in the professional literature of Christian education than I have. The books in this field which I have read have been instructive and stimulating, but my own specialized professional duties have kept me from using them as much as I should have liked. Even as a volunteer teacher in the church school I feel deeply the lack of thorough familiarity with curricular material of wide variety. As any other volunteer teacher should, I frequently consult with a local director of religious education or some other specialist for advice concerning curricular materials of various kinds, the needs of children at various ages, and technical aids to teaching.

I am a teacher of theology who has long been especially interested in the communication of Christian faith to "all kinds and conditions"—and ages—of human beings. Among church school teachers and other Christian educators I find everywhere such a hunger for deeper understanding of the Christian faith, related meaningfully to the teaching task, that I have been encouraged to attempt some assistance in this field. Perhaps specialists in religious education will not think such an effort by a theologian too presumptuous if they are fully aware—as I think they all are—how vastly inclusive the task of Christian education is and how essential it is to everything with which the church is concerned. There is room in this exacting and inclusive work for people of many specialties, each contributing his part to the whole.

It is in the spirit of collaboration in a common task that I have written this book. My purpose is not to set right the specialists in religious education. It is to supplement and assist them in their task and at the same time to help the ministers and teachers responsible for Christian instruction in local churches.

The assistance I am seeking to give is of two kinds.

First, out of many years devoted to theological study, I hope to present the Christian message in terms understandable in the present day and relevant to the present teaching task. This is a kind of assistance urgently needed by many. It is, of course, very important to know *how* to teach. It is even more important to know *what* to teach and *for what purpose*. Countless teachers, of many regions and denominations, have expressed need for more instruction in these matters. The questions what to teach and for what purpose are theological questions. As a theologian concerned and experienced with teaching at all age levels, in local churches and elsewhere, I believe I have a responsibility to give the best answers I can to these questions.

Second, I will point out some ideas about the resources, emphases, and methods of Christian teaching suggested by theological study of the Christian faith itself. I hope that specialists and other teachers can find among these suggestions some that are worthy of development and use beyond my competence to relate them.

I

The Proper Focus of Christian Education

THERE HAS BEEN MUCH THOUGHT GIVEN TO THE QUESTION, WHAT should be at the center of the Christian educator's attention, determining the purposes and method of his work?

A. Various Recent Theories

1. *Content-centered*

In many a European church and in some American ones, young children are put through a hard course of study centered in a catechism. Every child is equipped with a long list of questions and answers which must be memorized. A minister or other teacher takes up a few of these questions at each class session and "explains" each answer. The children are then drilled in repeating, on command, the printed answers in the exact words given and in "explaining" these answers in ways similar to those they have heard from the teacher. Often the pupils who answer most quickly and in language most nearly like that used in the printed literature and the teacher's "explanation" are praised or otherwise rewarded.

In such classes the content of the printed catechism controls the teaching process. The immediate and guiding purpose is to implant in the child's memory the questions and answers of the catechism and to teach him to repeat the answers and to explain these answers whenever called upon to do so. Often the teacher supposes that the children truly understand the answers because they are able to "explain" them, whereas in many instances

14

the "explanation" is little or no clearer to the child than the printed answers so carefully memorized.

In many American Sunday schools the Bible, rather than a catechism, is the all-controlling content. Both the effectiveness of the teaching and the success of the pupils are judged by the quantity of the Bible's contents transmitted into the children's minds and especially into their speech. The ability to repeat many Bible verses accurately; to find quickly passages announced by book, chapter, and verse; to tell the Bible stories and to answer quickly many questions about the book and the personalities introduced in it—these are often regarded as the proofs of successful instruction.

Here again, though with more breadth and variety, a given body of ideas and, to some extent even of words, determines the whole course of the teaching.

It would be easy to gain an exaggerated idea of the uniformity and rigidity of such practices. Actually, even when content is central and mostly controlling, a good teacher who loves children may vary procedures and introduce all kinds of ideas and enriching experiences not outlined in the printed material. Moreover, the teacher may also spend other hours with the pupils on the playground, at social functions, or in private conversation, when the expressed needs and interests of the pupils largely control the process.

Whether variety of approach is introduced or not, there is much to be said for content-centered teaching if the content used is so rich and important as the Bible. The Bible was written by many kinds of persons in many different moods. Even with young children its imagery occasionally makes vivid contact so that real communication takes place. More often this occurs in the lives of older children, youth, and adults. Moreover, the supplying of the memory with selected Bible passages provides a rich treasure house from which gems may be drawn for comfort, for guidance, for moral courage, or simply for apt expression on many later occasions. If the printed Bible is important to the church—and few would deny that—

then the great passages from the Bible indelibly etched in human memory are of incalculable worth.

Nevertheless, more is needed—much more. Often passages taught are not understood at all. Words memorized without at least partial understanding are unlikely to be useful in the future. Even with understanding, most pupils make little transfer of ideas from one situation to another unless positive help is given to that end. Verses and ideas encountered in a Bible class at Sunday school are likely to have little effect on actions or attitudes on a playground, basketball court, date, or selling job, unless taught with explicit, purposeful awareness of their relation to the life situations.

2. *Life-centered*

In response to the weakness of content-centered religious education, many specialists have stressed pupil-centered or life-centered [1] teaching. Paul H. Vieth wrote, in 1929,

The present emphasis on a life-centered curriculum of religious education grows out of a dissatisfaction with the results which have been achieved by religious teaching. For a long time we have been saying that book-learning is not enough. The attainment of knowledge as an end in itself is not the aim of education. Pupils learn to do by doing. We must go beyond instruction to the development of attitudes, ideals, purposes which have their fruition in character and conduct.[2]

Adoption of "life-centered religious education," says Vieth, will effect "two changes in our attitude toward our work." First, it will change *"The way in which we conceive our ends.—It will shift our emphasis from things learned to character achieved."* [3]

Second, it will change *"Our conception of the way in which*

---

[1] Some religious educators would distinguish the two, making "life-centered" a broader, more inclusive concept. Because it is the richer and more defensible term, I choose to use it here.

[2] *Teaching for Christian Living* (St. Louis: The Bethany Press), p. 55. Used by permission.

[3] *Ibid.*

life changes are brought about.—A life-centered religious education lays emphasis on learning to live by living." [4]

Vieth was obviously drawing upon the insights of John Dewey and his associates concerning educational psychology and method, and was seeking to apply these insights in Christian education. However, in doing so he spoke of "living," whereas Dewey spoke of "doing." Vieth rightly saw that Christianity involved much more than doing.

The writers who introduced and spread life-centered religious education made an incalculably important contribution to the church. Most of the best to develop in Christian teaching in the intervening years owes much to their insights and their enthusiasm. [5]

Both Vieth himself and others, like William Clayton Bower, later broadened and deepened the idea of life-centered Christian instruction in such ways as to give it much more specific Christian meaning. [6] The influence of the original impetus has continued in many other channels, alongside the work of Vieth and those closest to him.

However, the result has not all been good. Ideas have a way of being tested in history. It is especially true that if partial or one-sided ideas are made central, then, even if they are good, they tend to become exaggerated in their one-sidedness and distorted in application. This has been true of life-centered religious education.

Vieth placed considerable emphasis upon the important place of subject matter, especially the Bible. He said, though he did

---

[4] *Ibid.*, p. 58.

[5] For an example of a book written from a very different viewpoint, yet owing much to advocates of life-centered religious education, see Iris V. Cully, *The Dynamics of Christian Education* (Philadelphia: The Westminster Press, 1958), especially chaps. vi and vii.

[6] See, for example, Vieth's statement of the aim of Christian education in his book, *The Church School* (Philadelphia: Christian Education Press, 1957), p. 17. It will be noticed that the thought of this statement is drawn largely from James D. Smart, known especially for emphasis on "the Word of God" as central in religious education. Cf. Bower, *Christ and Christian Education* (New York and Nashville: Abingdon-Cokesbury Press, 1943), especially pp. 38-39.

not stress, that the pupils needed to be brought into a relation with God, and he elaborated on the importance of the church's providing the environment for Christian nurture. Others showed much less balance. Indeed, as one finds Christian education advocated in some books, it is difficult to see what makes it "Christian," rather than simply education, or, at most character education.

If the main principle determining what and how to teach is the life of the pupils and especially their own felt needs and interests, the educational process may, indeed, make them grow, but their growing in Christian faith and life may be highly questionable. They may grow in other directions. To be sure, the educational process is never altogether unguided, and all religious educators agree that it should be guided. But what is to be the guiding principle? How shall teachers and preparers of materials determine what kinds of growth are to be cultivated and what kinds should be discouraged? What is the norm and goal of growth?

This question is a theological question. It is really the question of the meaning and purpose of human life itself. On this question Christian faith affirms an answer different from Buddhism or American humanism. Christian education can hardly be truly *Christian* education without placing this distinctively Christian understanding of the goal somewhere near the center.[7]

3. *Group-centered*

One weakness of life-centered religious education, as it has sometimes developed, is its placing of the pupil, as an individual, at the center of concern. As many have pointed out, child-centered education is likely to produce a child-centered child.

[7] For an example of "Christian education" which can scarcely be recognized as Christian, see Ernest Chave, *A Functional Approach to Religious Education* (Chicago: University of Chicago Press, 1947). Highly relevant to the issue here being discussed is Harrison S. Elliott, *Can Religious Education Be Christian?* (New York: The Macmillan Co., 1940). While deeply dissatisfied with Elliott's answer, I commend his candid and clear facing of the issues.

Part of the goal of Christian education, it has been often recognized, is teaching the individual to be an integral and loyal member of the groups to which he belongs. To be a decent member of society, let alone a Christian, he must learn to subordinate his individual interests and desires to the well-being of the groups in which he lives. Human society would be a thoroughly disordered and continuous conflict were there no family loyalty, team spirit, patriotism, or human concern for mankind. Hence, some religious educators have stressed the need for centering attention, not merely on individual needs and interests, but also on group process and the relations of individuals to the group.[8]

4. Church-centered

However, there are many kinds of groups for many different purposes. There are even various kinds of grouping used in Christian education. At the same time, Christian education is a work of Christian people working together *as* Christians. Indeed, it is a function of the particular kind of group known as the church. Nearly all planned and continuous Christian education, even when carried on in families, is planned and promoted by organized churches. All Christian education is a work of the church in the larger sense including the whole body of people who are united by Christian faith—however sadly divided otherwise.

Moreover, Christian education, it may well be contended, should seek to induct the pupils into responsible participation in the life of the church. It is properly church-centered in that purposive sense.

There are many advantages in describing Christian education as properly church-centered. The church is something concretely experienced in life. It is a richly meaningful community including all the dimensions of human concern and divine-human relations which are included in the whole meaning of

[8] An early study of group process in religious education is Harrison S. Elliott, *The Process of Group Thinking* (New York: Association Press, 1928).

the Christian life. To emphasize the church is to stress the truth
that the whole church is, for good or ill, involved in the educational process. There are other advantages.

I have no quarrel with the idea of church-centered religious
education, so long as the church is conceived in sufficiently high
and yet experiential terms of genuinely Christian life. The
principal dangers inherent in the concept are a deadening in-
stitutionalism and a turning of the church in upon itself. To
be truly the church, the church must be forgetful of itself, and
even more forgetful of its formal institutional embodiment,
while being preoccupied with its Lord and the world's need of
him.

The idea of "church-centered" religious education was much
discussed in the Curriculum Study Committee of the Division
of Christian Education in the National Council of Churches
while that committee was preparing the ground for the co-
operative program of curriculum preparation in which many
churches have subsequently participated. The dangers were
widely recognized and yet most of us who commented in the
committee meetings on the idea of church-centered focus did
so with appreciation. The dangers can be surmounted and the
idea, like each of the others we have encountered, is an exceedingly useful one.

B. Different Meanings of "Focus"

The attentive reader may have noticed that the four answers
to the question of focus which we have examined actually answer different questions. All have suggested guiding principles
in the building of curriculum and in teaching. But the guiding
principles have been sought in response to different specific
problems.

Theories of content-centered religious education stress the
materials, especially the ideational materials of instruction—
whether in catechism or the Bible. Life-centered advocates at
first presented their views in stating the *purpose* of religious

education as approved kinds of "character and conduct." [9] Later both Vieth and Bower stated the purpose in terms of commitment to Christ and other specifically Christian objectives, while the idea of life-centered teaching came to be used to insist on the need for making the Christian message constantly *relevant* to present experience and need.

Group-centered instruction has not been suggested for the primary purpose of forming groups, but rather to stress the group *process* and *setting* of effective Christian instruction and development. Sometimes the group is stressed also in order to make clear that the true Christian objective is not finally individualistic, but implies a whole network of relations among persons. This is especially true when the group specified is the church.

It can be seen, therefore, that the various views we have examined are mutually exclusive only in their more extreme forms. One might acknowledge the purpose of Christian education in such a way as to include recognition of all the ideas we have discussed. Christian education would then be described as the nurture of Christian commitment and character, in the Christian church, by teaching the true Word of God through use of the Bible and catechisms or other church manuals, in constant relevance to life as experienced and including much group process. One could not, it is true, bring together without modification all the various emphases in one theory and practice. Yet we should acknowledge that in the best Christian education important truths and values of the various theories must be properly used.

C. Christian Education Centered Upon Faith in God

No great task like Christian education can be adequately guided by a slogan. Indeed, even the most expertly and carefully developed system of guiding principles when put to work will soon need, in the ever-changing course of human affairs, to be supplemented and corrected.

---

[9] Cf. quotation from Vieth above, p. 16.

I do not presume to have disproved the theories briefly discussed nor do I seek to displace them or other views not discussed. I have sought only to suggest the context in which I can make another proposal, for supplementation and, as I see it, a significant and needed change of perspective in relation to which all the rest may be given important and proper place.

It is imperative to affirm and emphasize the absolute centrality in Christian education of Christian faith in God.

The meaning of such faith and some of its implications for the purpose and method of Christian education will be discussed in the chapters which follow. So also will various reasons for this emphasis. Just now it is sufficient to warn that Christian faith in God does not mean only or primarily a list or system of beliefs about God. If it did we would be facing only another form of content-centered instruction.

1. *God the true center of Christian focus*

Jesus is reported to have said, "Seek first his kingdom and his righteousness" (Matt. 6:33). Likewise, when asked what was the greatest commandment,

Jesus answered, "The first is, 'Hear, O Israel: The Lord our God, the Lord is one; and you shall love the Lord your God with all your heart, and with all your soul, and with all your mind, and with all your strength'" (Mark 12:29-30).

After that, but only after that, he enjoined the love of neighbor. In the Christian life everything begins with God.

The central point from which all directions must be taken for the nurture of Christian life—and that is Christian education—the central point, the magnetic pole is God. Human experience may be badly distorted, human interests misguided, and human needs hidden under shells of self-deception. Only as the teacher's own heart and will are established first in God, as lessons lead to God, as God commands, judges, forgives, and sends out the pupils to serve him by ministering to other human beings, only then may genuine Christian nurture be accomplished.

The central and all-inclusive task of Christian education is teaching our Christian faith in God.

2. The goal

The true goal of Christian education is relating the pupil to God in glad, obedient faith. This *relationship of faith* must be our primary concern.

Such faith implies a whole constellation of other personal relationships and concerns. The Christian is to love his neighbor as himself. This involves him deeply in the joy and the need of every neighbor, obligates him to forgive every neighbor, makes him servant of all.

These human relationships cannot be taken for granted in Christian education. It will not do to suppose that we have only to bring the individual in his solitary need to God, with assurance that he will then make right all his human relationships. Explicit, careful guidance must be given in the tangled human complexities of our time. But all must be viewed in relation to God.

Human relations cannot simply be taken for granted once faith in God is established. On the other hand, human relations cannot be made right apart from faith in God.

3. Context and Resource

The faith relationship is not only the primary goal of Christian education. It must be seen also as offering the most vital context and resource of the whole process. As I shall try to make clear later, the work of religious instruction must itself be regarded as an expression of faith in God.

Faith in God does not exclude other contexts and resources. Indeed, it requires them. For example, it requires use of the Bible; relevance to life and its needs; and the teaching, praying, worshiping, working community of faith, the church.

Yet it is necessary to place right at the center of all this and to stress in radical fashion the Christian faith in God. All life, all true Christian character, all proper development of the church, and hence all Christian education begin, continue, and come to fruition in him.

II

The Meaning and Message
of Faith

A. New Testament Teaching on Faith

THERE ARE SEVERAL MEANINGS ATTACHED TO THE WORD FAITH (Greek *pistis*) in the New Testament. All have something to contribute to our proper understanding.

1. *Faithfulness*

The primary meaning of the word for faith used in the original Greek of the New Testament (the noun *pistis*) is faithfulness or reliability. It is thus closely related to the adjective *pistos* meaning faithful or reliable, a word often used to describe God's trustworthiness (as in I Cor. 1:9).

When the word *faith* is used in the New Testament to signify the steadfast faithfulness of the Christian, it usually carries also other meaning besides this. Nevertheless, this meaning is important. A good example is found in the question asked in Luke 18:8: "When the Son of man comes, will he find faith on earth?" Another is in Paul's words to the Thessalonians, "Therefore we ourselves boast of you in the churches of God for your steadfastness and faith in all your persecutions and in the afflictions which you are enduring" (II Thess. 1:4).

2. *Trust*

More often the meaning is turned right around so that instead of indicating the faithfulness or worthiness of a person to be trusted it means the attitude of a person trusting such a one.

Especially is this usage predominant in the first three Gospels. In these Synoptic Gospels, the word occurs twenty-nine times and in twenty-seven of the twenty-nine instances it means trust or confidence. When Jesus pointed out people's troubled anxieties about material things, resulting from their lack of confidence in God, he described them as being "men of little faith" (Matt. 6:30). After healing a sick woman, Jesus said to her, "Daughter, your faith has made you well" (Luke 8:48). When Jesus saw the efforts made by the friends of a paralyzed man to bring him to Jesus, showing their great confidence in the Savior's healing power, Jesus "saw their faith" (Mark 2:5) and proceeded with the healing.

In Paul's writings faith usually includes the trust, but the most emphatic meaning in his typical usage is different.

3. Total commitment

When Paul spoke of faith, he usually meant the kind of active trust in which a person commits the whole meaning, purpose, and destiny of his life to Christ. Of course this faith must be enduring and it must involve trust, so it includes the meanings already discussed. But primarily it is an entrusting of all one's hope to the promise of life through Christ.

The trust implied is not that of a person who sits with folded hands and peace of mind because he is confident that everything will turn out all right. It is better symbolized by the attitude of the deep-sea diver who, trusting his equipment and supporting crew, drops into the sea and explores the ocean floor.

Yet it is more than this. The diver may regard the significance of his life and even the soundness of his decision to go down into the sea as assured even if the air hose may, in fact, become fouled, causing his death. The risk is a sound one, even if it is a risk. Faith in Paul's sense is total. In faith the Christian stakes his all, even the very meaning of his existence, as well as his life, happiness, and hope, upon the action of God in Christ.

This total commitment of life to God, in trust and steadfast loyalty, is the distinctive and full meaning of Christian faith. Every other meaning is subordinate to this.

4. *Believing*

Faith as characteristically represented in the Gospel of John and in the three epistles by the same name means the act or state of believing.

The noun *faith (pistis)* does not appear at all in any of these four books excepting the first epistle where it appears only once. There are no other books in the New Testament in which the word does not appear. On the other hand the verb, *believe (pisteuo)* occurs ninety-six times in the Gospel of John alone!

This is not altogether an accident of personal usage. To the writer of the Fourth Gospel, the idea of faith in the Pauline sense was altogether familiar and he accepted it heartily as shown in John 14:1 and other passages using the phrase *believe in (pisteuo eis)* followed by the name of God or Christ. But to the Fourth Evangelist it was especially clear that every act and every moment of faith in this sense of total commitment was an implicit affirmation of a belief. To believe in Christ, entrusting all one's very being to him, is to assert the truth of the proposition that Jesus Christ is the Son of God, that God so loved the world that he gave his Son for our salvation, and various other doctrines. This writer saw the critical issue between the Christian and the non-Christian as the question whether or not all such affirmations are true. The typical meaning of the verb *pisteuo* is precisely to believe as true. Often in the writings ascribed to John the evangelist this characteristic meaning is put beyond question by following the verb with a clause introduced by the conjunction *that (hoti)*. This construction was also sometimes used by Paul, and, of course, in the same sense, as, for example, in Rom. 6:8: "We believe that we shall also live with him."

5. *Doctrine believed*

Occasionally a further development of thought occurs, so that the noun *faith (pistis)* means, not faithfulness, trust, total commitment, nor the act of believing, but the body of doctrine believed. Thus Jude wrote, "I found it necessary to write appealing to you to contend for the faith which was once for all delivered to the saints" (Jude 3).

Here faith means, not the relation of the committed believer to God but the teaching or message which, when believed, makes the relation of loyal, trusting, total commitment possible.

B. Relationship and Message

The goal of Christian education must always be to establish and nurture the pupil in faithful relationship to God. The true purpose of the teacher is not merely to implant a body of doctrines in the pupil's mind, nor even to win his acceptance of them as true. It is to win the total commitment of his life to God in grateful, obedient, trusting service.

Such commitment, however, is not won merely, or primarily, by commands or exhortations. The *commitment* of faith is possible only when the pupil has heard and believed the *message* of faith.

We can trust God only when we see how he loves us. We can be grateful and glad in his service only when we know what he has done and will yet do for us. We are able to be faithful to God and serve even the most faithless men with steadfastness only when we learn of God's steadfast faithfulness to us.

The commitment of faith does not follow automatically in response to the message of faith. But the message alone makes the response possible.

If religious education is Christian, then, it must communicate the message, with clarity and persuasiveness.

What, then, is the message of faith?

C. The Message of Faith

1. *The Bible*

The message we teach is, of course, derived primarily from the Bible. The biblical teaching has been elaborated and supplemented through further revelation by the Holy Spirit to the

Christian Church through the centuries. Our message has even been supplemented by experience in the secular order. The sciences and the serious thought of mankind have contributed to the whole body of wisdom in the context of which we understand the message of the Bible. Even though some Christians might have misgivings about these suggestions of supplements to the biblical revelation, most Christians would agree that at least the message of the Bible is taught today in such a context of wider experience that in the planning of our teaching we must consider the history of the Church and our present cultural situation.

It is necessary that we give instruction concerning the nature of the Bible, something of the history of its development, and the character of its authority. Although it may introduce difficulties, the history of biblical times should be taught. In Christian education we are much more concerned with the teaching of the Bible relating to God's purpose for our redemption than with its teachings on scientific and chronological matters. It is also apparent that Christians do not regard every part of the Bible as having the same kind of authority for us. Even those who would believe that everything stated in the Bible is true and valid would nevertheless take account of the fact that some of the teachings in the Old Testament have been so displaced or fulfilled in the teaching and work of Christ that they have not now the same kind of practical authority to guide our lives which the ancient Hebrews believed them to have for themselves.

We need to teach our people how to read the Bible.

Every part of it should be read in the literary context within which it stands. Often the understanding of the historical situation in which a passage was written throws important light upon its meaning also; hence historical context is needed.

All of us as Christians would believe that the whole Bible should be read in the context of our own relationship to Jesus Christ. If Christ is Lord, then he is Lord of our understanding

of the Bible and its authority, as well as being Lord over all
other aspects of our living and thinking.

The Bible must be read seriously if it is to be truly understood. The reader should think of himself as standing in the
presence of God, seeking to understand the will of God for him.
He needs to read with the intent to do what he finds God com-
manding him to do.

The Bible needs to be read also within the Christian fellowship, so that each person's understanding may be criticized and
supplemented by the understanding of others.

Finally, none of us reads the Bible in a mental vacuum. All
of us bring to it some of our knowledge and powers of understanding, even the peculiarities of our various languages. This
is not to be regretted, for God has spoken to us here within
our earthly context and not within some heavenly realm. However, it does require that we should be aware of our own cultural heritage and that our own interpretation should be corrected by the understandings of people who have lived in
different kinds of cultural situations. We should read it in
the fullest possible human context.

The supreme importance of the Bible for us comes from the
fact that it is through the Bible we know the gospel. The climax
and heaviest emphasis of our biblical instruction must be on
our teaching of the gospel of redemption by grace through faith
in the Lord Jesus Christ.

2. God

In the ancient book of Deuteronomy there appears the teaching known to the Hebrews as the *Shema:* "Hear, O Israel: The
Lord our God is one Lord; and you shall love the Lord your
God with all your heart, and with all your soul, and with all
your might" (Deut. 6:4). Jesus emphatically confirmed this
teaching.

God is one. No other objects of supreme adoration are to be
tolerated in his presence. Not only the ancient Hebrews and
certain primitive peoples of modern times, but highly sophisti-

cated people also, do serve other gods. To be sure, these other gods are no gods; they are idols. Yet there are people whose very lives are devoted to the securing of wealth, or fame, or prestige in the eyes of their neighbors and friends, or the pursuit of pleasure. All these are idols. The Lord our God is one Lord and nothing else is to be made an object of supreme devotion. Whenever there is a clash of loyalties between our devotion to God and his will on the one hand, and any other object or purpose whatsoever on the other, God must rule if we are to be obedient to the great teaching of the first commandment in Christ's own designation.

God is the creator of all things. He himself is not created. He is from everlasting to everlasting. He alone is an absolute being requiring nothing else to explain or support his own existence. He is sufficient to himself.

As creator, God reigns over the world. No other power can stand before him. In the end his power is sufficient for the accomplishment of his will. This teaching is terrible and inacceptable to those who wish to work contrary to his will. However, it is a great comfort to those who place themselves in his hands, ready faithfully to obey him. God has committed some of his power to human stewardship. This power is often terribly misused. It may seem at times that other forces are very strongly against the faithful and that they are fighting a losing battle. However, we know that God is sovereign and he will have the last word.

God is holy. The original meaning of the Hebrew word translated as "holy" implies a fearsome, mysterious, transcendent God. He is to be approached with awe and even with fear. This is taught in innumerable ways in the Old Testament, as, for example, by the narratives of people who were injured or killed by trifling with things closely related to God. It is taught also in the elaboration of rules for preparation to come into his presence. Much biblical symbolism and imagery is devoted to emphasizing the awful otherness of God. We are told, "The fear of the Lord is the beginning of knowledge" (Prov. 1:7). This

is a hard saying to many people of our times who believe that
there should never be fear of God but rather only trusting love.
Does not the New Testament teach that perfect love casts out
fear? Are we not commanded to love God with all our heart,
mind, strength, and soul? Yes, it is noteworthy that fear is the
beginning of knowledge, not its end. But it is doubtful whether
anyone can ever come truly to love God without having first
feared him. We do feel the shudder of fear when we stand in
the presence of truly stupendous physical power, such as a
thunderbolt, an earthquake, or a hurricane. How much more
should we tremble in the presence of him who is the source of
all such powers and many others besides!

The holy God is also perfectly righteous. He is the author of
the moral law and he himself can be counted on to be just.
Indeed, in the prophetic tradition of the Old Testament the
holiness of God is often interpreted in relation to the righteousness of God. God is distant from us and awe-inspiring to us,
not only because of his vastly superior power, but also because
he is perfectly righteous, whereas we are sinful.

Indeed, God would be unapproachable were it not for the
fact that he loves us. It is because of his steadfast mercy that he
has arranged for the children he has created to know him and
to approach him. The God who has created us and all the world
in which we live is also the God who has made his love known
to us in Jesus Christ.

God is far above us and far beyond the world which we see
about us. In the language of theology, he is transcendent. On
the other hand, God is never far off; he is available to us anywhere and everywhere. He speaks in the inner heart. We cannot
go anywhere to escape either his judgment or his pursuing love.
He is not only transcendent, but also immanent.

Both the Old and the New Testament are much concerned
with the question why there should be so much evil in the
world which God has made and over which he is sovereign. In
the Old Testament the problem relates especially to Israel, his
chosen people. In the New Testament it relates principally to

Jesus Christ, who was his beloved son, but who nevertheless suffered an ignominious and suffering death upon a cross. There is also some attention paid to the persecution and suffering of the primitive Christian community. Why should these things be in God's world?

In both the Old and New Testaments the probing of this question resulted in some of the deepest and highest disclosures of God's purpose. The prophets of the Exile discovered that suffering is not always given as punishment for sin, but is sometimes accepted by the innocent for the sake of redeeming the sinner. Suffering may have a cleansing power and through suffering may come a higher triumph than would be possible without it. In the New Testament this is seen more clearly in the life and death of Jesus Christ. At first Paul thought it was utterly impossible that one whom God had chosen as Messiah could possibly suffer the death of a criminal upon a painful cross. However, when he confronted the risen Lord on the Damascus road he knew that this was God's way. He never ceased to wonder at it and he never succeeded in explaining it. However, he did know that God used the suffering and death of his faithful son for the redemption of mankind.

We are not today able to explain very well why there should be so much of suffering and death in a world which God created and over which he is sovereign ruler. Nevertheless, looking to Jesus we can accept our ills with patience and faith, knowing that he suffered the ultimate pain and sorrow of human life, freely taken upon himself for our sakes. Some aspects of this marvel may be explained in various ways by different ones among us, but in the end we all confront the mystery of God's wondrous love and wisdom, beside which the highest intelligence of man is but foolishness.

3. Man

According to the Bible, God made man in his own image. Despite the vast chasm of difference which lies between man and God, there is also the positive relatedness of the Creator with created persons, between the heavenly Father and his earthly children. It is the high privilege of human beings to show forth the likeness of God. This likeness is tragically disfigured and often altogether hidden from view by sin. Nevertheless, God has implanted in our very nature the deep hunger and need for him. However much we seek to fulfill life's meaning through the quest of other values, we can never find rest and completion until we find our rightful destiny in the likeness of God himself.

Man, as we see him around us and most of all within ourselves, is not the creature that God intended. We are fallen deeply into sin. Not only do we actually make choices which are not in accordance with his will, but the basic orientation of our lives is not what he purposed for us. Human beings are prone to serve their own selfish interests. God intended that we should be devoted to serving his eternal purpose in loving and faithful obedience. The strong tendency toward sin which is evident in human life today is due in part to the human situation. Being finite creatures and given freedom to choose between good and evil, we are tempted by that very discovery of our freedom to try it out and to learn its full extent. This is the disastrous desire to be "like gods."

Then too, when we first come to moral consciousness, we are already burdened by habits formed in the innocence of infancy and early childhood, habits which are now hard to break. Likewise, we are burdened today by the customs, examples, and other profoundly evil influences of past generations. Every generation of human beings, with some reason, blames its difficult predicament on the preceding generation. We begin life already very much involved in the vast network and power of evil. Yet underneath all this strong tendency to sin, there is the deep human restlessness given by our Creator which makes it impossible for us to be contented with a life on terms other than those of obedience to him.

Man is mortal. All of us are doomed to die. It is one sign of the sickness of our age that people are extremely reluctant to face the fact that they must one day die. We conceal this fact in many ways and yet deep within ourselves we know, even from early childhood, that we are mortal. This is not a fact which is evaded in the Bible; rather it is plainly faced and is dwelt upon at considerable length in both the Old and the New Testaments. This is part of biblical realism.

Until it is recognized more clearly than most present Protestants are prone to see that we stand before the judgments of God as condemned sinners who are about to die, we cannot appreciate with anything approaching adequacy the meaning of the gospel of redemption. For what we are offered in Christ is salvation both from condemnation for our sin and also from death.

4. *Jesus Christ*

The Scriptures bear abundant witness that Jesus is both Son of Man and Son of God. The two books in the New Testament which emphasize most the unique divinity of Jesus Christ, namely the Gospel of John and the Letter to the Hebrews, are also the books which lay the greatest stress on the humanity of Jesus.

It is exceedingly important that we acknowledge properly both that Jesus was a man and that in Christ God was reconciling the world to himself. If we neglect the humanity of Jesus in our teaching, we not only pervert the Gospel; we also put him beyond the reach of our people so that they cannot see in him the one after whom they are to pattern their lives. Neither can they see in him the assurance that within this vale of sorrow and sin, a pure life of perfect obedience to God can actually be lived. It is precisely in Jesus the man that God pronounces judgment upon our sin.

However, the gospel is not only good news of man; it is also good news of God. From the vast darkness of mystery and death which enfolds us and our world, there has come the clear and glorious Word of God declaring to us his wondrous love and power. Until we see what God was doing in Christ, the New Testament accounts give us only human aspirations which might become the way to disillusionment and despair as we find how impossible it is for us to live by the standards of Jesus. When we see the love of God in the work of Christ, we are then and then alone given hope and strength by which to live in faithfulness to him.

Central in Christian worship and thought is the cross of Christ. The cross must be seen constantly in close relation to the life and teachings and resurrection of Jesus. Hundreds of human beings have suffered agonizing death upon cruel crosses. All bear terrible witness to the cruelty of which man is capable and many bear witness also to the courage and fidelity of human beings. However, only one cross is the cross of our redemption; that is the cross of Jesus. Separation of the cross from the person of Christ must not be permitted in our interpretation.

It is precisely the Jesus Christ who not only spoke the Word of God but who was the Word of God made flesh, that suffered death upon the cross for our reconciliation to him. How is this reconciliation accomplished? Here again we confront much mystery. We must begin with the fact. The New Testament gives abundant testimony to the reality of the reconciliation accomplished through the cross. Likewise, the testimony of innumerable men and women in subsequent centuries declares the great fact that by faith in the cross of Christ reconciliation is accomplished.

We may go further and see that at the cross both the contemptible sin of human beings like ourselves and also the amazing love of God are made manifest. The disclosure of our sin might lead us only to despair, but seeing our sin against the background of God's forgiving love, people who dwell at the foot of the cross find themselves brought to true repentance. God waits eagerly for that repentance and his forgiveness is the marvel of marvels to those who receive it.

Through the centuries theologians have endeavored in many different ways to explain how the cross brought about our reconciliation. Some figures of speech are suggested in the New Testament—the ransom from slavery, the sacrificial lamb, the high priest making the offering which is not repeated but is once and for all. All of these symbols are highly suggestive, and some have been highly elaborated in later Christian thought. Yet all leave open for our experience and meditation the deeper understanding of this supreme sacrifice which Christ made upon the cross for us.

5. *The Holy Spirit*

We worship God not only as the eternal creator and judge, God the Father Almighty, maker of heaven and earth; and as the Son gloriously revealed in Christ Jesus; but also as the living Holy Spirit who speaks to us in the silence of our own individual hearts and also in the community of worship and work where faithful men and women join together in the name of Christ.

The entire work of Christian education may be properly regarded as an expression of faith in the Holy Spirit. The real teacher who must be principally depended upon for the work of Christian instruction is indeed the Holy Spirit. The human being who is called the teacher is only a witness through whom the Holy Spirit may work his will. To be a good witness requires all the love and skill of which a human being is capable. Even more, it requires faith in God as present counselor, the Holy Spirit.

The work of the Spirit is represented as varied. The Holy Spirit reminds us of Jesus Christ and the wondrous work Jesus has done for us. The Holy Spirit convicts us of our sin. He illuminates and directs us as we pray earnestly for guidance and place ourselves in his keeping. He emboldens us to speak and to act in obedience when courage is required to do so. He works before us, beside us, and after us to make our witness effective. He gives us comfort and knits our hearts with those of other believers, forming the sacred community which is, in the highest sense, the Church. He meets us in prayer and communes with us in hours of joy which need no ulterior purpose.

Someone may ask, "Are not all these things the acts of God

himself?" Yes; precisely. This affirmation is a part of the essential meaning intended by the doctrine of the Trinity. The doctrine of the Trinity was not devised by men who sought to divide God into three parts. Rather, this doctrine is a way of affirming that the God known in his richly varied revelation to man is one indivisible God.

Particular interpretations of the Trinity have differed from the beginning of its enunciation until now. From the beginning it has been stated ambiguously. "One God in three persons" has suggested to some people a collective noun referring to a little society of three separate individuals. However, this is far from the meaning of any classical statement of the doctrine. Indeed, the word "persons" or *"personae"* when originally employed in this connection was itself an ambiguous word referring to roles in a drama *(dramatis personae)*, rather than to separate individual people. On the other hand, the word was already coming to be used sometimes to mean individual people. The term was especially useful because it was not very exact. Men could not sufficiently understand the relations between God the Father-Creator, the Son as seen in Jesus, and the Holy Spirit as experienced in power, to define these relations with precision. This remains true today.

6. *The Christian life*

The Christian life cannot be taught by any human teacher. It is not primarily an attempt to follow certain moral principles, while giving assent to various doctrines. Neither is it a system of habits and attitudes in which a child might be drilled. It does include characteristic habits and attitudes, but not such as are capable of being imposed by drill.

The Christian life is a life lived in those relationships to God and neighbor which God has made possible by the wonderful gift of his love to us in Jesus Christ.

We can and must bear witness to that gift. We must also assist our students to become aware of their desperate need for it. We cannot teach their actual acceptance of God's forgiving love in Christ; but we can help them understand what is offered and how the gift may be accepted. We can help guide the student into the worshiping community in which he can be further prepared. The decisive event of faith itself occurs in relationship between God and the individual.

The need for human instruction does not end with the acceptance of Christ by faith. There continues to be acute need of more information, shared wisdom, and guidance concerning the understanding and expression of the Christian life in all aspects of our existence.

The Christian life is characterized by faith, that is the total commitment of self to God. This implies various beliefs about God and about oneself, but it is more than belief. It implies obedience to God's commands, but it is also more than obedience. It is the casting of the self utterly upon his mercy in surrender and the living in complete dependence upon him for the very meaning, reality, and fulfillment of one's existence.

The Christian life is characterized also by hope. This hope is more than earthly. It is not dependent upon the headlines in the latest newspaper. It rests upon the good news of the gospel. Since God is for us we can face the future not with fear, but rather with assurance.

Finally, the Christian life is a life of love. This love is grateful response to God's own love. "We love, because he first loved us" (I John 4:19). It is a deep communion or participation (Greek: *koinonia*) with God in the sharing of his treasure, "the unsearchable riches of Christ" (Eph. 3:8). It is also a grateful and openhearted reaching out to share this treasure with other children of God.

This love is reckless in its self-giving. Yet it is studious and careful in concern for the precise needs and perils of every neighbor. This concern requires conscientious study and instruction regarding many kinds of neighbors, far and near, and their many relationships to us—personal, political, economic, churchly, and cultural.

7. *The Church*

The Church of Jesus Christ was formed by the Holy Spirit, drawing together in fellowship (Greek: *koinonia*) the people called out (Greek: *ekklesia*) by God's love freely given in Christ. It is the people of the New Covenant, as Israel was the people of the Old Covenant.

The Church is entered by repentance and faith. Since the Christian life is a life of love, every Christian is inevitably drawn out into fellowship with others. The voluntarily solitary Christian would be impossible. The Church is called to transcend every earthly barrier of race, class, and nation in witness to one Lord and one faith.

The same love and faith which draw the Church into being also compel it to carry its testimony to the world. The very nature of the Church is its divine commission to share the good news of Christ with all people, in every aspect of life.

The Christian mission is the task of the whole Church. The mediation of Christ's love to every one for whom Christ died —that is, to every human being—is the task of "the people of God." In this New Testament sense, all believers constitute "a royal priesthood" (I Pet. 2:9). As Christian educators we have the urgent task of making clear that the Church's mission to the world is the sacred calling of all Christians, laymen as well as clergymen. Indeed, if the mission is to be fulfilled in most places—as in factory, home, business, or agriculture—it must be through the Christian ministry of laymen, because they are the only ones with the specialized skills and responsibilities, and they alone are *there*.

The New Testament provides also for specialized leadership in the Church. Our various traditions have deeply divided us in our understanding and practice of the relations between ministers, in the narrower sense, and laymen, while the question of episcopal supervision is always at hand to divide us further. We shall be concerned with instructing our people in these matters according to our various convictions, while we continue to search for further light.

We are increasingly aware that this task has been poorly done. As recent interdenominational studies of the seminaries show, many theological students enter seminary with radical misunderstandings of the office for which they are preparing. There are also new evidences of a wide gap between the views held by laymen without specialized religious training and by professionally trained ministers concerning the responsibilities of Christian laymen.

It is also needful that we teach much better, than we have been doing in most of our churches, the meaning of worship and the particular modes of worship in our churches. Especially important for most of us is careful instruction concerning the sacraments. If our laymen are to participate in them fully, with faith, they must learn to understand them better than most of them now do.

Probably none of us would regard the Church of Jesus Christ as identical with the particular denominational organization with which we are affiliated. Even the Roman Catholic Church acknowledges that there may be members of the true Church who are not communicants of that institution and who may even oppose Roman Catholicism, if they are kept from actual submission to Rome only by "invincible ignorance." We need to face directly the whole problem of relating our denominational churches to the universal Church of Christ, the true "holy catholic Church," and to one another, and to assist our people in the most careful, humble, and responsible thinking on these matters.

8. *History and last things*

In the Occident we seem instinctively to think of history as having direction and meaning. We sometimes fail to recognize how largely this assumption is due to Hebrew and Christian teaching, although some Greek philosophy, especially Aristotle's, has also contributed to it. It is not a universal human assumption. Some peoples have little sense of time or history at all, while others think in terms of great returning cycles.

While there are expressions of a cyclical view in Ecclesiastes, the Bible as a whole emphatically teaches that there is a divine purpose within or above the course of history, giving to it meaning and goal. Isaiah, for example, wrote: "This is the purpose that is purposed concerning the whole earth; and this is the hand that is stretched out over all the nations. For the Lord of hosts has purposed, and who will annul it?" (Isa. 14:26-27.)

The Bible teaches that we have come from God's own creation and move toward a final consummation in which Christ will reign victorious in judgment and in love. There are many conflicting theological interpretations of the way in which God's purpose is to be fulfilled. The differences are rooted in different presentations of the matter in the New Testament itself. Whether the reign of God is to be consummated through God's use of human instruments or by intervention cutting across all the human processes of history; whether little by little or all at once; whether by spectacular visible events or by spiritual inward change; whether within history, outside history, or at the end of history; all may be persuasively argued on different biblical premises.

However, Christians agree that God will win the victory; to trust in him is to be assured of fulfilling our rightful destiny as individuals and to participate in his accomplishment of his purpose for mankind.

God's kingdom is not limited to this world. The resurrection of Christ symbolizes and witnesses to God's power and purpose to raise from death to life all who are united with him. The life which God offers to us begins here and is everlasting.

III

Sequence of Instruction

HOW MUCH OF THE MESSAGE AND RELATIONSHIP OF FAITH SHOULD be taught in the nursery? What part is suitable for primary children? What must be left for the instruction of older youths or adults?

These questions represent the problem of sequence.

While not professing adequate specialized training in educational psychology to confront this problem, I believe I do have something important to say about it. Such questions must not be left wholly for solution by educational psychology. The message of faith itself has something to say about them. In the end I believe there is no ground for quarreling between a true understanding of the message and a true educational psychology. However, the message does require us to adopt a different perspective than would be held by people without the message. There is danger lest this perspective be neglected. The present approach to the problem of sequence will be from the message of Christian faith. The attempt will be made to show how this approach can be supplemented by the technical insights of genetic and educational psychology.

A. The Whole Faith Presented at Every Age Level

1. *All need the benefits of God's saving acts*

The Scriptures give no suggestion that the gospel is especially for adults although, to be sure, the Bible was written by adults for adult readers. Indeed, we are warned that only as an adult becomes "as a little child" can he hope to be saved. Yet this does not mean that the gospel is for children only.

If for life that is life indeed and for life eternal all are dependent upon all that God has done for us in Christ, then the whole of God's gracious work is for all and all are in need of it. There are no exceptions. But note that this is very different from saying that all the *ideas* or *words* of the message are for all ages.

Soon it must be said that the meanings and benefits of God's redemptive acts are not conveyed to all in the same way. Different channels and methods of communication must be used to bring these benefits to different ages. But first it must be emphasized that the church is bound to bring them to all.

When Jesus commanded that little children be allowed to come to him and when he "took them in his arms and blessed them, laying his hands upon them" (see Mark 10:14-16), it was made clear to all who would believe in him that even little children needed to be brought into his presence and to be blessed by him.

Everywhere, through all the centuries, wherever the church has baptized infants, it has declared that God has acted in their behalf, as well as for adults. The church celebrates God's act in giving to another child his saving grace through believing parents and through the larger family, the church. In baptizing infants the church also acknowledges its solemn responsibility, as the parents acknowledge theirs, to nurture these little ones from earliest infancy to Christian maturity. This nurture is Christian education.

2. *Not a one-sided bit, but the fullness of the faith relationship needed*

Often the meanings and treasures conveyed by the message are divided up and bits are parceled out to children of various ages, according to their supposed needs and abilities. In this procedure the truth is recognized that not all *ideas* of the message can be taught to every child; indeed, no ideas *as ideas* can be taught to tiny infants. But realities are more important than the ideas which represent them to the intellect. Christian education is primarily concerned with the realities for which ideas and words are only signs.

The whole range of the reality of God's dealings with men needs to be brought to all, even little children. We are not to bring only sweetness and light to the young with judgment withheld until later. All is to be brought in ways relevant to the child's capacities, but all is to be brought.

The tiny infant born of Christian parents is already receiving benefits of the gospel through their faith, their obedience to God, and their freely released love. He does not understand this priceless gift, nor even know that his life is different from that of other babies born of parents who have not received assurance of God's forgiving love, nor become channels of his grace.

If his own parents have received a distorted gospel, then the infant, too, is being distortedly nurtured. It may be that the parents think of God as a harsh tyrant who is ready to pounce on every mistaken act or erroneous belief as a reason to send them to hell. Their lives are then bound to show some of the hardness and rigidity of living in fearful awe of such a God. Their child will be more sensitive to this than any other person and he will be injured or deprived by it until someone else can mediate to him God's forgiving mercy.

On the other hand, the parents may think of God as only love with no judgment. Perhaps they have listened to preaching about peace of mind presented in such soft and easy terms that they regard God and his commands with neither awe nor obedience. Their soft self-indulgence may be reflected in impatience with the child who interferes with their all-important pleasure. It may be expressed in an immature, indulgent, dependent love which tends to stunt and warp the child's spiritual development.

In one way or another the message of faith which the parents have heard, together with their response to it, will begin to be communicated to the child from his very birth—perhaps, indeed, even before his birth. As the child grows, the channels of communication become broader and more varied and persons other than parents become increasingly involved.

Regardless of channels and persons the communication of the whole sacred treasure of the faith is needed at every age.

B. Method and Depth According to Capacity

One message, but changing language

The Christian message is one for infant and grandparent, for kindergartner and theological scholar. The languages by which the message is communicated are all the languages of mankind. These include not only the tongues of the various nations and tribes but also the many other signs and symbols of communication—gestures, caresses, frowns, smiles, laughter, helping acts, intonations of voice, work, tears, departures, songs, groans, rhythmic play, gifts, deprivations, silence, and many others.

Words are usually signs of ideas and the ideas are intended to represent realities. But realities are often communicated without words or ideas as when a week-old infant is quiet while his sleepy, but concerned father holds him in his arms, but starts crying again as soon as he is placed in his crib—however comfortable and warm.

When we speak of education, even religious education, we often think immediately of instruction by words and ideas only. Since few ideas can be taught to very young children, churches sometimes suppose that anyone who can properly guard the health of little children is a suitable person to be in charge of the nursery. Actually, the nursery is potentially a vitally important part of the church school. Moreover, however advanced may be the education of youth or adult, the nonverbal and even nonideational means of communication continue to be of incalculably great importance in the further nurture of his Christian life. Words and ideas are not the only means of teaching the commitment and relationships of Christian faith,

At the same time, the words useful in the adult class may be highly unsuitable in the kindergarten, and likewise the gestures or acts by which the message is communicated to primary children may be disastrously inappropriate in the high-school class.

The real objective must continually be kept in view. That is the nurturing of faith as a real personal relationship to God, involving all other relationships as well. Words and ideas are more or less appropriate to this task of nurture, depending on the age, previous experience, and present mood of the pupil.

C. Some Guidelines of Sequence

Can theology give any suggestions regarding the communicating of the faith at the various ages? Yes, I believe that when supplemented by a little study of human beings at the various ages, theology can offer some valid guidelines.

1. *Adults, mediators of faith to infants*

As already indicated, infants and very young children are affected chiefly by their relations with their parents and other adults. These adults must mediate to the young child the blessings of their own relation to God.

2. *The message in the kindergarten*

Watch a child in the kindergarten. He is eagerly looking, feeling, listening, exploring. He is also grasping, crying, laughing, shrieking in anger, and showing his fondness for people and toys winning his favor. Shall we try to teach him theology?

Actually we cannot avoid it. We can only decide *what* understanding of God and man we should teach and how well. Of course he should be taught in ways suitable to his stage of development. Consider what this means in relation to the various topics presented earlier as the message of the Christian faith.

What shall he be taught about the Bible? It may make little difference whether he is taught to sing songs about the Bible, repeat verses about it, memorize texts from it, or do none of these things. Most children of this age are not doing much abstract conceptualizing. Nevertheless, they are relating images and learning attitudes toward them. We shall not, therefore, expect to teach the kindergartner such doctrines about the Bible as were stated in the preceding chapter. On the other hand, if we ourselves read and handle the Bible in his presence, with attitudes appropriate to these beliefs, and if we are in loving relationship with him, we shall be teaching him such attitudes —that is, reverence without idolatry, wonder and expectancy without fetishism or superstition, gratitude and joy without complacent familiarity.

Some writers have claimed that it is useless to try introducing children of four or five to God, because their conceptual powers would not yet permit them to think an idea so abstract as the idea of God. But such a view is based upon the highly dubious theological doctrine that a little child never encounters God himself in reality.

It would be an absurd presumption to try instructing anyone, of any age, about God if we could not believe that God himself had spoken to the student before us. But we may confidently believe that he has spoken and will speak again. In the church-school kindergarten we can arrange situations in which the child's need and love and wonder are so stimulated and directed that he will be open to God's own presence. The child may not, at this age, be able to know very much about God. But he can have something much better than such knowledge. He can know God himself even while not knowing his name. With such knowledge by acquaintance he can also learn to associate both the name and the experienced presence of God with the highest values of beauty and love he knows and with attitudes of proper fear, thankfulness, and reverence. He is not yet capable of mature faith with all its rich meaning and disciplined obedience. But even in the kindergarten his heart and mind can be opened to God's presence. In this way he is being prepared for the understanding, full commitment of faith later.

Similarly, the child will not yet learn doctrines about man. But he is becoming acquainted with actual people. It is important that he know people who can make him aware of high human possibilities, as sustained by the grace of God. He should have the privilege of knowing some people who can truly mediate to him the love of Christ. They should also teach him of human frailty and divine and human forgiveness by showing that in the Christian church people readily admit their own mistakes and such sins as pride or impatience, without despair and with ready forgiveness. In such ways the child comes to know the image of God in man and the reality of sin in context with the forgiveness of sin. Here again *cognosco* (I am acquainted with) precedes *intelligo* (I know conceptually). The child can know God before he can think or talk about him, much as he knows his mother before thinking or talking about her—or about anything.

Similarly, we can tell simple stories of Jesus and little children, while we ourselves mediate his love; we can show pictures of Jesus and speak of our grateful love toward him. We have already been speaking of the Holy Spirit in discussing the introduction of little children to God. In all this nurture of the child's acquaintance with God and the cultivation of generous, loving attitudes and actions, we are at least prefiguring the child's experience of the Christian life. All this is happening in the Christian fellowship and so the child is learning the meaning of the church, not in concepts but in experience. Even concerning eschatology the principle holds. To be sure, the child does not now experience the "last things" of death, the future life, or the consummation of God's kingdom. Yet he is sometimes afraid. If his teacher trusts in God and expresses, therefore, an indomitable confidence and hope, especially in moments of crisis and of prayer, the Christian hope is being mediated, in an initial way, to the child.

One mistake often made is to suppose that the kindergartner does not need theology and therefore any well-intentioned person who likes little children, especially if pedagogically resourceful, can handle the kindergarten without having received careful Christian instruction or developed mature Christian character. This is a serious error. Having taught during recent years in church-school kindergarten, adult, and senior-high-school departments, I should say that the kindergarten made as great demands on my theology, as well as on my faith, as has the adult class or the teen-agers. The demands at the three age levels are of radically different kinds, but I cannot say that any one requires either more or less understanding of the gospel. Let no one underestimate the importance of a sound beginning of Christian instruction in the earliest years of life or the depth of the demand which such instruction makes on the teacher.

On the other hand, it is a temptation to suppose that because the whole Bible may have been "covered" in the instruction given in the elementary school years, the studies in high-school years and later may as well be devoted exclusively to current problems and variously selected issues of special interest. This, too, would be a grave mistake. The longer I teach at senior and adult levels, the more firmly convinced I am that the *whole* message must be taught again at each of these levels, almost as if it had never been taught before—almost, but not quite, for care must be taken to choose new approaches, thus avoiding a deadly repetition. So new is the emotional, volitional, and ideational context at each of these levels that the gospel itself is likely to appear now as a great mystery and even novelty. This, of course, is because the true mystery of the gospel is, at every point, far beyond the highest human capacity for full understanding. Hence to each age level it offers its own new dimensions of adventure.

3. The primary years

As the child begins his studies in day school, his ability to express ideas in words expands rapidly. This is a time for many simple stories, songs, guided play, simple construction with blocks, drawing, and other expressive activities.

Here, too, despite the growing use of words, little should be expected from efforts to give connected accounts of the biblical message or of the teacher's faith. Even when stories are told, the moods and personal relationships conveyed are of primary importance, while ideas and words are distinctly secondary.

Prayers, briefly and simply spoken, are of increasing importance through the primary years. It is especially important that prayer be real, authentically expressing attitudes appropriate to the situation—gratitude if the group is happy, repentance if relations have been strained or angry, sorrow and need if there has been a shock of bereavement or a disappointment.

4. *Junior and intermediate departments*

As children are moving into the fourth grade it is about the right time to begin a connected presentation of the Bible and its story. At the same time there must be much illustration and comparison of biblical events with present life, to make them meaningful to the boys and girls.

In the intermediate (junior-high-school) years similar work may be continued, but with increased emphasis on the message underlying the biblical history and so with increased stress on present conditions, especially present problems confronting youth.

At some time in the junior or intermediate years there should also be a forthright urgent challenge to the youth to commit their lives in faith to Jesus Christ. We do not become Christians simply by growing up under Christian instruction and gradually getting more mature. Each person must be, as Jesus said, "born anew" (John 3:3). He must decide for himself to give his life to God, trusting God's disclosure of himself in Jesus Christ. Unless that happens his earlier childish wonder in God's presence will be stifled by devotion to false gods and at best he will live only in the reflected glow of a secondhand religion. This is right and proper in infancy, but in older youth and adults, to have nothing more is to be lost.

5. *High-school years*

High-school students are becoming acquainted with the wide world of history, science, and public affairs. Some of them are having their first love affairs—a few of which are lasting. All are beginning to see before them the years of adult responsibility. Many are changing personalities so fast they hardly know themselves. Decisions made earlier may now seem scarcely to have been theirs.

If decisions for Christ have been made earlier, they may not now be taken for granted. The challenge to decision must be made again and again in the context of the new vision of meaning, the new sense of self-identity, the new personal relationships and the dawning awareness of coming responsibility.

Many teachers of high-school youth approach them as mainly fun-loving youngsters without serious thoughts. Few mistakes are more serious. Teachers who only cater to their love of good humor and recreation will lose their respect and accomplish little. This is an age of deep perplexity and disturbance. It is an age calling for appeal to the very depths of yearning for God and eternal life, of capacity for heroic courage and response to the call for sacrifice.

The message is now to be set forth in this context. The youth may not feel free to express their real need. They are likely to encourage their teachers to play around on the surface with them. But they need now to know what the Bible really has to say to modern man in his materialism, selfishness, prejudice and fear. They need the message of redemption from sin and death. Some will turn away from it, but more will respond to that message than to anything else that the church may offer them and those who respond with decisions of faith begin to provide a new dimension of Christian earnestness in many a church.

6. *After high school*

Beyond the high-school years there remains much to be learned. Young people who go to college face new intellectual doubts and new temptations. They also face wonderful new opportunities. They need the message of faith interpreted and re-interpreted in relation to this widening frame of reference.

Whether in college or not, after high school most youth soon show whether they have become personally committed to Christ or have only been "going along" with parents or other youth in the neighborhood. The challenge to renewed decision to face the new issues and responsibilities of their present life in the light of Christ as Lord must be made afresh.

7. *Adults*

Even in adult life there is no such thing as standing still in Christian development. If there is no advance, there is retreat. Without renewal of God's grace and accompanying spiritual growth, there is inevitable deadening of faith and slumping into the spiritual indolence which is sin.

The great difficulty of teaching adults arises from their great variety of situations, responsibilities, education, spiritual development, and present capacity. Yet here, too, there is in all persons a need for the message of faith in its depth and in all its variety of relevance to the different situations and needs of life.

Adults must be stimulated to take a larger part in instructing themselves through study, personal Christian work, and discussion—especially discussion of the relevance of the message to their own special responsibilities in family, office, factory or farm work.

Lay adults are the great secret weapon of the church in its battle for righteousness and faith in the world. It is mostly unused because few adults have learned what they are called to do and therefore must and can do for God in the world. This hidden power must be released if the church is to go forward. The releasing is mostly the task of adult Christian education.

D. Campbell Wyckoff well says that "in childhood the emphasis is likely to be more on perceiving the gospel, in youth on accepting it, and in maturity on discovering and meeting its ever-changing requirements." [1]

[1] From *The Gospel and Christian Education* by D. Campbell Wyckoff, p. 109. © 1959, W. L. Jenkins. The Westminster Press. By permission.

To this excellent statement I would only add here that between the perceiving in early childhood and the accepting in youth must come considerable understanding or conceiving. This supplementing of perception with conception, that is of experienced reality with thoughtful ideas, is introduced mainly in the junior years (fourth through sixth grades).

IV

The Christian Doctrine of the Triune God

THE HEART OF CHRISTIAN EDUCATION IS FAITH IN GOD. THIS faith is a personal relationship of grateful, obedient commitment of the whole self to God. The development of such a relationship supports the development of a proper understanding. The reality of faith supports the doctrine of faith. More important for the teacher, however, is the fact that right teaching or doctrine about God helps to sustain and develop the right kind of relationship to him.

The message of Christian education therefore has at its heart Christian teaching about God and to this teaching more attention must be given. If the teaching about God is balanced and reasonably thorough, a proper understanding of man, his proper destiny, the way of salvation, the church, and other matters of special Christian teaching will follow readily.

Through the centuries of Christian history the symbol and safeguard for the wholeness and correctness of teaching about God has been the doctrine of the Trinity. Where this doctrine has been neglected the understanding of God has tended to become one-sided and some of the rich heritage of our faith lost.

It is especially fitting that the doctrine of the Trinity should be brought into renewed emphasis in Christian education, for the careful formulating of the doctrine was itself a product of Christian education. L. Millar has written an excellent little

book entitled *Christian Education in the First Four Centuries*,[1]
which tells of the great educational task confronting the ancient
church as it moved out from its earliest Jewish environment
into the wider world of predominantly Greek culture. One
of the most effective Christian educators of the second century
was Clement of Alexandria, whose work Millar especially praises
for its "almost phenomenal success," and for his writings about
teaching, which "remain the most precious contribution made
by the early Church to the educational theory of the race." [2]
Clement was especially sensitive to the variety and richness of
God's revelation and sought to gather together and organize
this rich heritage for purposes of instruction. He writes, "there
is one river of Truth, but many streams fall into it on this side
and on that." [3] It was to preserve the main streams of this
heritage in one understanding of God that the doctrine of the
Trinity was formulated in the second to eighth centuries of
the Christian era.

A. Reasons for Emphasizing the Trinity

It may seem strange to some teachers that I should devote
four chapters of a book on Christian education to discussing
the doctrine of the Trinity. I do so because I regard this doctrine
as being of utmost relevance and importance for the most
urgent, practical work which the Christian educator has to do.
There are, of course, other ways in which a Christian may properly speak of God. But there are three special values in the
trinitarian formulation of our faith in God for Christian education today.

1. *Corrective of distortions*

The doctrine of the Trinity is the best corrective for some
of the most serious distortions of the Christian faith in contemporary theology and religious education.

Theology has often tended to ride particular hobbies. Its

---

[1] London: The Faith Press, 1946.
[2] *Ibid.*, p. 66. Used by permission.
[3] Quoted in Millar, *ibid.*, pp. 63-64. Used by permission.

course of development, like that of psychology and some other disciplines, has tended to be a zigzag between various one-sided extremes. I know of no means for correcting this tendency toward distortion and narrowing of emphasis in theology equal to the doctrine of the Trinity.

Now religious education, especially in recent years, has been deeply influenced by theological developments. When theologians have become one-sided in their emphasis, often it has required many years for the influence to be deeply felt in Christian education, but the influence has come and religious education has become seriously one-sided, also. Fortunately, the church as a whole, with all its traditions, institutions, and liturgies, has partially corrected such distortions and Christian education has rarely gone as far afield as some theology of the current or preceding period. Nevertheless, I believe that Christian education has been in the recent past and is today seriously affected by distortions in theology. I believe that the doctrine of the Trinity is an exceedingly useful instrument for correcting such distortions.

2. *Summary of Bible message*

A second reason for emphasizing this doctrine in a book such as this is one I have learned by an experience in religious education itself. Within the last few years I sought to work out in my mind a little book which would state the total ageless message of the Bible in the simplest terms possible without distortion. For this purpose I had to find the elements in the Bible which were most emphatic and which were most relevant to all human life; hence, the elements which were most important and also most teachable. When I had outlined my little book with these thoughts in mind, I was somewhat surprised to find that a doctrine of the Trinity was emerging as the basic outline of the book. If you wish to see how this happened, you may observe for yourself in the book which has since been published and which is entitled *The Enduring Message of the Bible*.[4]

---

[4] New York: Harper & Row, Publishers, 1960.

3. *Clues for Christian education*

A third reason why I have chosen to emphasize the doctrine of the Trinity in this present book is that this doctrine provides some especially important clues for the philosophy and method of Christian education. I must ask you to wait patiently for the elaboration of this theme at later points in the book. First we need to see, in brief, the origins of trinitarian doctrine; some contemporary theological views concerning it; the relation between the doctrine of the Trinity and the outlining of the biblical message in its simplest, basic elements; and finally, some ways in which the doctrine of the Trinity serves to correct certain theological aberrations which are contemporary with us.

B. Early Development of the Doctrine of the Trinity

1. *Sources in the Bible*

The history of trinitarian writing must begin with the New Testament; yet the relevant passages there, while suggesting such doctrine, are exceedingly sketchy and often statements are made which are in rather severe tension with trinitarian doctrine as formulated by the church at later times.

Many New Testament scholars believe that one of the earliest examples we have of the teaching in the primitive church is the sermon of Simon Peter recorded in the second chapter of Acts. In this sermon Peter speaks of "Jesus of Nazareth, a man attested to you by God with mighty works and wonders and signs" (Acts 2:22). Notice the formula: *Jesus, a man, attested to you by God.* This does not sound trinitarian. However, we come much nearer to a doctrine of the Trinity in some of the closing words in the sermon. Here Peter says, "Being therefore exalted at the right hand of God, and having received from the Father the promise of the Holy Spirit, he [Jesus] has poured out this which you see and hear" (Acts 2:33).

A more explicitly trinitarian statement, probably formulated much later, occurs in Matt. 28:19, where we read the familiar words, "Go therefore and make disciples of all nations, baptizing them in the name of the Father and of the Son and of the Holy Spirit." These words probably reflect a very early use of a trinitarian baptismal formula, yet this by no means implies the sort of elaborate trinitarian doctrine which was to develop later. Nothing is said here about *hypostases, personae,* substance, or *perichoresis*—words much emphasized in later teachings on the Trinity. Probably the best-known sentence in the entire New Testament conveying trinitarian ideas is the benediction by Paul, reading, "The grace of the Lord Jesus Christ and the love of God and the fellowship of the Holy Spirit be with you all" (II Cor. 13:14). But notice how far these words are from conveying the thought of a strict trinitarian as defined by later church councils. Here the "Lord Jesus Christ" on the one hand, and "the Holy Spirit" on the other, appear to be contrasted with "God," whereas a self-conscious trinitarian would regard the three equally as God.

Furthermore, there are other passages in the New Testament which seem to be in conflict, or at least in tension with a doctrine of the Trinity. For example, in the third chapter of II Corinthians, verse 17, where the context shows unmistakably that the phrase "the Lord" refers to Christ, the statement is made "Now the Lord is the Spirit." It has been commonly observed that many Pauline passages would seem, if taken alone, to imply a binitarianism (belief in two in one) of the Father and the Son rather than a trinitarianism of Father, Son, and Holy Spirit.

If, with R. S. Franks, we speak of "the first anticipations of the doctrine of the Trinity in the New Testament," we must also speak of "its definitive formation in the patristic period." [5] Of course, non-trinitarians persist among the earlier church fathers. For example, in the second century Hermas subscribes to a binitarian doctrine in which the pre-existent Christ and the Holy Spirit are regarded as identical. According to Franks

[5] *The Doctrine of the Trinity* (London: Gerald Duckworth and Co. Ltd., 1953), p. 60.

the first mention of God as three occurs in the work of Theophilus when he "speaks of the triad (*trias* in Greek), God—His logos and His wisdom." It is no accident that this passage occurs in the work of a Greek apologist who was among those most heavily importing Hellenistic ideas into the interpretation of the Christian faith. For it was in confronting the Greek philosophical world that the church began to express its faith in the more elaborate formulas of doctrine.

The first use of the Latin word *Trinitas* occurs in Tertullian's work entitled *Against Praxeas*. Since in some of its later developments the doctrine of the Trinity has often been regarded as threatening the belief in the unity of God, it is particularly interesting that Tertullian, when he wrote this work and first used the term "Trinity," was himself a monarchian, that is one who especially emphasized the unity of God as a single individual. He was, in fact, defending one form of monarchianism against another. It is also significant that Tertullian's doctrine was what is known as an economic doctrine of the Trinity; that is, he based the doctrine upon three kinds of functional relationships within God, rather than distinctions of substance.

We cannot here follow the intricate arguments concerning the Trinity through the Arian heresy, Athanasius' victory over Arianism, the stress on the "threeness" of the Trinity in the Cappadocians, or the formulations of successive church councils. The writer generally regarded as having stated most exactly the classical orthodox doctrine of the Trinity is John of Damascus, who died near the middle of the eighth century. The heart of John's teaching on the Trinity appears in the following affirmation, from *The Exposition of the Orthodox Faith* (Chapter 2) :

We, therefore, both know and confess . . . that God is One, that is to say, one essence [ousia]; and that He is known, and has his being in three subsistences [hypostases], in Father, I say, and Son and Holy Spirit; and that the Father and the Son and the Holy

Spirit are one in all respects, except in that of not being begotten, that of being begotten, and that of procession . . . [6]

That John of Damascus was especially concerned with safe-guarding and emphasizing the unity of God is made evident in many passages, among which is the following:

We believe, then, in One God . . . one essence, one divinity, one power, one will, one energy, one beginning, one authority, one dominion, one sovereignty, made known in three perfect subsistences and adored with one adoration . . . united without confusion and divided without separation (which indeed transcends thought) .[7]

A historian of the doctrine of the Trinity, R. S. Franks, well says, "There is no doubt that the final emphasis in the Greek doctrine of the Trinity is on the Unity of God." [8]

The doctrine of the Trinity was, in fact, a means by which the early church maintained a belief in one God while at the same time affirming that God was truly revealed as he is, both in the Old Testament revelation of the creator and judge of us all, and also in the disclosure of God through Jesus Christ, and finally in the experience of the power of the Holy Spirit in the early church and the early Christian individual. The fact that a doctrine of the Trinity as such was first formulated by a mon-archian, Tertullian, symbolizes the fact that the doctrine was intended to safeguard the unity of God while maintaining the richness of Christian experience. Such formulation was made necessary by the threat of various heresies which either denied altogether one or another of the biblical revelations of God or separated them, and so moved toward an outright tritheism or even polytheism. The formulation was also made necessary by the demands on Christian education in the Hellenistic world.

[6] Philip Schaff and Henry Wace, editors, *A Select Library of Nicene and Post-Nicene Fathers of the Christian Church*, 2nd series (New York: Charles Scribner's Son, 1899) , Vol. IX. Translated by S. D. F. Salmond.

[7] *Ibid.*, Chap. 8.

[8] *Op. cit.*, p. 121.

The Christian beliefs simply had to be formulated in a system of doctrine which could be taught in that cultural environment.

C. The Doctrine of the Trinity in Contemporary Theology

In the present world one can distinguish several main tendencies in regard to this historic doctrine.

1. *The doctrine renounced*

First there is the movement to renounce it altogether. This tendency occurs not only in some of the more radical liberal theologians, especially avowed Unitarians, but also in such men as Wilhelm Pauck and Cyril C. Richardson. To be sure both of these men would subscribe heartily to some of the purposes for which they believe the doctrine of the Trinity was originally formulated, but the formulations themselves they think to have been a failure, or at least to be lacking in persuasiveness and clarity to the modern mind.

2. *Emphasis on the Three*

A second trend, to be found especially in Anglicanism, is the movement toward a more radical differentiation of the Three within the One. This movement is typified by Leonard Hodgson, one of its more extreme spokesmen. We may call this type of teaching the social theory. Rooted in the teaching of the Cappadocian Fathers in the sixth century, this modern view moves even closer to an unguarded tritheism. As representative of it we must associate with Leonard Hodgson the name of the distinguished Roman Catholic theologian Charles F. D'Arcy.

3. *Stress on unity*

More characteristic of recent trinitarian developments is Karl Barth's teaching that we should speak of God in his unity as a person and designate each of the three as a mode, not a person. Barth is not being critical of the fathers who spoke of God in three persons; he is only pointing out that language has changed and in the modern languages the word "person" and its equivalents have come to mean a personal individual quite unambiguously and clearly. It did not have this meaning when the doctrine of the Trinity was being formulated. Barth hastens to add that although the three modes came to be known through three modes of revelation, we are not to look behind these three for a hidden fourth—the real God who has not been revealed. The God who has been revealed to us as Father, Son, and Holy Spirit truly is what he is disclosed to be. With all this I find myself in hearty agreement.

However, it is disappointing to turn from this explicit teaching of Barth on the Trinity to his work as a whole. Barth's theology is barely trinitarian. So extreme and exclusive is his emphasis on God's revelation in Jesus Christ that he comes close to denying any revelation as Father and as Holy Spirit. To put the matter accurately, he would claim that God is actually revealed to us as Father and as Holy Spirit only in Jesus Christ. Consequently we may say that in spite of Barth's emphasis upon the three modes of revelation as the key to understanding the doctrine of the Trinity, he himself usually regards God as having three modes of *being* with only one mode of *revelation,* namely that in Jesus.

We might better regard the doctrine of the Trinity as a compact, symbolic summary of the history of Christian revelation. At the same time we should wish to say, of course, that the God who is revealed as Father, as Son, and as Holy Spirit truly is what he is revealed to be. In this sense the three modes are not only modes of revelation, but modes of his very being. This does not imply that there is in any sense a separation or discrete individuation of the modes within his own nature.

D. The Doctrine of the Trinity as an Outline of the Biblical Message

At the beginning, I indicated that the doctrine of the Trinity was a cryptic symbol of the whole biblical message in outline. I must now expand this thought.

1. *Three universal human questions*

The late philosopher, Edward G. Spalding, said that there were three great questions which human beings in every age must ask. One is "From what source do we come?"; the second is "Toward what goal do we rightly move?"; and the third, "Why?" The Bible is devoted to just such basic questions. However, the question of the source from which we come and even more the question concerning the goal toward which we move are answered in such a way in the Scripture that there is no need to ask the third question—"Why?" Rather, the imperative final question for the person who receives the biblical message becomes, "How may I move from where I am to that great goal which God has purposed for me?" The three questions to which the Christian faith is an answer are, then, "From what source do we come?", "Toward what end do we rightly move?", and "How can we get there?"

As these questions are answered in the Scripture and in the teaching of our faith, the reply is trinitarian in structure. I do not mean simply that there are three answers to these three questions. I mean to say that the three answers are affirmations of the three modes of the Trinity.

2. God the Father

From what source do we come? From "God, the Father Almighty, Maker of heaven and earth." "It is he that hath made us, and not we ourselves" (Ps. 100:3 K.J.V.). We are not the result of some chance collecting of atoms. We were created by a personal being for his holy purpose. Before we existed, his love went forth to create children with whom he might share the riches of his own life. He made us in his image. Vast as must always be the separation of quality and power between God and man, nevertheless in important ways we are like him.

However, what we are is not what he has purposed. It is evident from the tragic mess in which we find ourselves, both socially and in our private individual lives, that somehow we have missed the way which he intended. So serious is the deviation of mankind from the divine purpose that every generation now finds itself battling a strong current running against righteousness and peace. It is this situation which is symbolized in the doctrine of the Fall. Not only do we come from God the Father in the sense that he created us, but also in the sense that we have come very far from him and profoundly need to return to the way which he had planned for us.

3. God the eternal Son

Toward what end ought we to go? God has made us for himself and we remain restless and discontented until we find our peace in him. But how are we to picture or understand the life which he intended for us? God has disclosed his will and way for us in the man of Galilee, Jesus of Nazareth. God the eternal Son, God the everlasting purpose for man is disclosed to us with marvelous beauty and purity in the life, death, and resurrection of Jesus Christ. Jesus is our supreme example. In so far as we fulfill the purpose of God, we shall show a spirit like his. It is the rightful hope and expectation of every Christian that one day, as Paul says, we too shall be like him.

However, Jesus is not only an example to be imitated by us. By the purity of his devotion, his sacrificial obedience to God, and his love of man shown on the cross, he has disclosed to us at once the wretched character of sin, even our sin, and the Father's forgiving love. Through this disclosure he has reopened the way which our self-righteous defenses tend to close. He enables us to repent with understanding and with genuine hope that God will truly forgive and restore us. At the foot of the cross we find ourselves stripped bare of all those shells which we erect around ourselves to prevent others and even ourselves from knowing our own wretchedness and need. At the foot of the cross we humbly ask God to forgive us and save us; not because we have been righteous, but because he has shown to us his forgiving love in Jesus. At the cross we learn also that the way of sacrificing love is the true way of reconciliation between one person and another. If the holy God uses no thunderbolt to make us obey, but rather condescends to humble and sacrificing love as the way of supreme disclosure, how much more should we humble ourselves in willing, patient, and devoted search for reconciliation with those who wrong us.

4. *The Counselor*

In the long road that we must travel between the creative hand of God and the ultimate goal of becoming like him and moving into his presence, we are not called upon to walk alone. There came in the experience of the disciples a day when neither the Jesus who had walked the paths of Galilee with them nor the resurrected Christ was any longer to be seen. Their outlook was full of foreboding and dismay. But in that time God sent to them another counselor and comforter, the Holy Spirit, to empower and guide them in the way that leads home. The historic doctrine of the Holy Spirit, so much neglected in the present generation of theology and preaching, is the symbol which has kept the church from becoming a mere archaeological expedition, celebrating a thing that God did in the long ago. The Holy Spirit is available today. God continues to speak and to guide his people. In the hour of trial, God can be called upon to lend his living presence and strength. He reminds us of what was disclosed to men long ago in Jesus; he renews our commitment; he shows to us that the life and love which were in Jesus are today in the everliving presence of God. The process of revelation continues today under the power of the Holy Spirit. Jesus is represented in the Fourth Gospel as having predicted that the counselor whom he would send would teach the disciples many things which he himself had not taught. The church needs to keep itself always sensitive, open-minded, eager, and ready to receive new truth which God may be seeking to give us through many different channels. For God the Holy Spirit continues to speak today and to lead his people.

It would be hard to find a doctrine which is more important to the church today than the doctrine of the Holy Spirit. Vast numbers of human beings are becoming aware today that the problem of mankind is far too great for men to solve alone. It is not enough that we were created by God originally, nor is it enough that one who lived over nineteen hundred years ago showed us the way, and died and rose again for us. There must be available today a divine power ready to help us. When we affirm that God does live and that he is available to each of us now we are affirming the doctrine of the Holy Spirit.

E. The Doctrine of the Trinity as Theological Corrective

The doctrine of the Trinity is especially helpful as a corrective of various one-sided views in theology. For in theology, as in some other enterprises of the human mind and spirit, there is a tendency for the pendulum of emphasis to swing from one extreme to another. The doctrine of the Trinity, expressing as it does the rich breadth of Christian doctrine, is exceedingly helpful in correcting this tendency to one-sided narrowness. This usefulness is evident in the present as in earlier times.

1. *Barren deism*

One tendency of theology is to move into a barren Unitarian deism. When the human approach to God is primarily philosophical and abstract, the tendency is to believe in a God who created the world long ago and whose will acts according to the universal principles of law; but also one who is distant and unconcerned as far as the individual and the concrete particular situation are concerned.

In the face of such tendencies to barren deism, the doctrine of the Trinity reminds us that God has made himself known at a particular time in history in an individual, Jesus Christ. In Christ we see the importance and meaning of God to us, not in terms that are abstract and general, but in terms that are concrete and vital in significance. In Christ we see God not as a general principle but as a personal being who loves and cares for us.

The doctrine of the Trinity reminds us also that, so far from being a general and abstract principle, God is a living Spirit, a power presently available to each of us, seeking us, responding to us, and communing with us, binding together in a community of faith all of those who believe and trust in Christ.

2. *Christomonism*

A second tendency which has been conspicuous in much recent theology is that toward a kind of Unitarianism of the second person sometimes spoken of among theologians as Christomonism. Those who represent this one-sided tendency say that God does not reveal himself in the world today and indeed has never revealed himself to man excepting at one point in the entire historical process. That one point, they say, was the Christ-event, that is, the incarnation, life, crucifixion and resurrection of Jesus. Such teaching takes such a low view of evidences of God's creative work and of the nature of man as he is at present in the world that Christian faith becomes almost irrelevant to issues of present decision. The common life of humanity is regarded as utterly estranged from God and separated from him by a gulf impassable by either the thought or will of man, even with the help of God. The common life is then in danger of being abandoned to a pagan secularism.

In the face of such teaching, the doctrine of the Trinity reminds us that we believe in God the Father Almighty, maker of heaven and earth. This is God's world. There are signs of his handiwork to be found in the heavens above, on the earth beneath, and even in the heart of man. However far man may drift from the course which God has plotted for him, he never can be altogether content with any way excepting that for which God has made him. The way to peace and security is the way of God; there is no other. The physical and social sciences, insofar as they are discovering the truth, are also discovering the truth of God. Christian faith, therefore, can join forces with the true insights of the sciences in learning the best approaches to our present personal and social problems.

Likewise, the doctrine of the Trinity reminds us that God is the Holy Spirit present with us. Even now he is seeking to give his guidance that our present problems may be solved aright. He is our great contemporary.

3. Humanism

The doctrine of the Trinity corrects also the badly perverted Unitarian doctrine of the second person known as non-theistic humanism. According to humanism there is no God but man.

It is man that we must serve. But this raises the question what kind of man we want to serve. Humanism vacillates between extremes. Sometimes it is a romantic sentimentalism which cannot see individual men for what they really are, but sees only a romantic man-in-general such as can nowhere be found. On the other hand, some humanists commend a dismal realism in which we would be resigned to serve our lowest passions and darkest desires. Neither sentimentality nor a crass materialism will do.

The doctrine of the Trinity reminds us that there is one man, a man of a particular kind; indeed, a specific person who represents to us a God worthy of our reverence. That one is Jesus Christ. The doctrine of the Trinity reminds us that man is not God but a creature of God, the creator and sovereign of all. This doctrine reminds us also that if man is to be saved today, it will not be by his own unrelieved human efforts, but rather by his humble and reverent cooperation with the Spirit of God before whom we repent and whose guidance we seek.

4. *One-sided emphasis on God as Spirit*

Theology, and more especially practical church life, is not altogether immune to a similar one-sidedness of perverted doctrines of the Holy Spirit for which we need the doctrine of the Trinity as corrective. One-sided doctrines of the Holy Spirit take three different forms. First there is a kind of dynamism which in our various pentecostal groups sometimes loses emphasis upon the person of Christ and then threatens to lose ethical anchorage, so as to become a search for emotional power for its own sake. Anyone who has observed the emotional orgy of a religious group seeking for psychic demonstrations of power without ethical content will know how dangerous and destructive such an emphasis can be. The dynamism and the power are sorely needed. Without God-given passion we can hardly hope to solve any of the greatest problems which confront us. The power, however, must be structured in our minds and wills by recognition of the way in which God has made us and by the ethical guidance of our knowledge of Christ.

A second form of overemphasis on the third mode of the Trinity occurs when such stress is laid upon subjective religious experience that religion becomes a vague and sentimental introspection. Many people could well use a greater concern about their own spiritual condition. However, when this concern takes the form of constant dwelling upon one's inner emotional state and when one is asking continually whether he sees in himself evidence of the presence of the Holy Spirit, this preoccupation is not likely to be useful unless accompanied by a strong and clear understanding of God's creation and of the ethical standards taught and exemplified by Jesus of Nazareth.

Third, there is the cult of togetherness. The Holy Spirit, as one can readily find in the New Testament, forged the community of faith into one body. The hard barriers which divided class from class, nation from nation, and race from race were broken down by the power of the Spirit and all became one in Christ. Being conscious of the wonder and glory of such a united community, many in our day have become preoccupied with a search for togetherness for its own sake. There are even churches in which all fellowship is thought mistakenly to be Christian fellowship. Community without purpose can quickly turn into hostility and disintegrate. Even while fellowship remains, it is a wretchedly empty thing if it lacks the inspiration and power of divine purpose. The doctrine of the Trinity reminds us that through the study of created nature and through the teaching and example and work of Christ we can learn a purpose which redeems community and makes it a victorious church of God.

F. Teaching the Doctrine of the Trinity

If, as Christian educators, we do adopt the historic doctrine of the Trinity as a theological corrective and as an instrument for assuring the wholeness of our teaching, should we also teach this doctrine to our pupils?

Assuredly, yes! The doctrine is useful because it is true. Both as useful and as true it is a great good which ought to be preserved in the life of the church. If it is to be preserved it must be taught.

The doctrine of the Trinity is taught in most of our churches in many hymns, as for example:

> Holy, holy, holy! Lord God Almighty!
> Early in the morning our song shall rise to Thee;
> Holy, holy, holy, merciful and mighty!
> God in three Persons, blessed Trinity.[9]

Likewise, in ritual it is prominent, especially in the sacraments of baptism and The Lord's Supper.

But to many laymen these uses are highly confusing or misleading because our people have received so little instruction in the history and precise meanings of the doctrine.

How, then, are we to teach the doctrine? Of course, the method must differ at the various age levels. Without trying to give a complete account, let us illustrate at certain levels.

1. *In the kindergarten*

All teaching in the kindergarten must be in the mode appropriate to the kindergartner with perception, emotional mood, personal relationships, and experienced activity taking precedence and with minor use of concepts.

Now, if we remind ourselves that God is Father, Son, and Holy Spirit, we will want to lead the kindergarten child into certain appropriate experiences relating him to such a God.

We will seek to stir his appreciation and gratitude for the gifts of God the creator. We will encourage his sense of wonder and mystery in growing things, the sky, his home and parents, the love which surrounds him. We will seek to provide him with considerable freedom, yet within an order where limits are firmly held to protect the rights of other individuals and the plan of the group as a whole. The teacher himself, by living a disciplined, punctual life of loyal devotion, gives the child an experience of knowing a person acknowledging God's rule.

[9] Reginald Heber.

Since God the Son is known principally and concretely in Jesus, the child will be shown pictures by which artists have sought to represent Jesus. He will be taught simple songs about Jesus and stories of Jesus' ministry. Believing in God as revealed in Jesus, the teacher gives assurance of God's forgiving love both by his own ready forgiveness and by his teaching about God.

One day in church school kindergarten my wife and I were supervising a period of varied activity when there were sudden shrieks of anguish and anger. Two little girls were in a violent quarrel and both were crying. When I went to them and asked the trouble, one looked at me ruefully through her tears, and said, "She said God doesn't love me; and God does too love me."

The other protested, "No, he doesn't; not when you are bad, and you were bad."

It was plain to see that some mother insufficiently instructed in Christian doctrine had been trying to use the wrath of God to punish her little child. I could not just now instruct the mother, but I had two angry and tearful little girls on my hands.

I brought them to a low bench, set one on either side of me and wiped the tears out of their eyes. Then I said, "Of course God loves you; he always loves you." Immediately there was a protest: "Even when you're bad?" I replied firmly, but happily, "Yes, even when you're bad." I was thinking to myself, "God shows his love for us in that while we were yet sinners Christ died for us" (Rom. 5:8).

Then I added, "God loves all his children. When you've been bad to one of them God is sad while he is still loving you. You want God to be glad while he is loving you, don't you?" Both nodded, and I said, "Now you want to be nice to each other and be good friends so God will be glad, don't you?" They nodded again, so I concluded, "Now God is glad. He loves you and he is glad because you are loving each other too."

Hand in hand they went off happy, to play together with a toy which one had previously pulled away from the other.

2. *In the junior department*

How would you teach the doctrine of the Trinity in the junior department? I should begin, I think, with the Trinitarian benediction. After all, these children are beginning to take a real interest in what goes on in church, and the minister pronounces a benediction, usually a Trinitarian benediction, in most of our churches. It may be for example, "The grace of our Lord Jesus Christ, the love of God the Father, and the communion of the Holy Spirit, be with you all." I would ask, "What does this mean?" We would talk about it very deliberately, having in view the wealth of meaning which attaches to each of the three parts of the benediction. Again, I would take a trinitarian phrase from a hymn of the church, like the phrase, "God in three Persons, blessed Trinity," and ask, "What does this mean?" I would have to use an analogy which would be rather crude because it is the best I could do, and because there is no analogy which will adequately represent the Trinity, especially to a fourth-, fifth-, or sixth-grade child. My analogy might be this: "When we talk about God as three persons, we mean that God is in three different roles. He is one God, but he is in three different roles, and we know him in these three different roles. You know about the roles in a play." I would illustrate this.

"Now," I might say, "here is a man by the name of Mr. Smith who happens to be an usher in the church. He is also a banker and he is a golfer. Some people know him in church; they see him as an usher all dressed up, coming down to the altar to receive the offering; they think of this man as a churchman. Other people have never been to the church where he is a member and do not know that he is an usher, but they know him as a banker in a bank. And somebody else may not know him either place, but knows him only on the golf course. Someone mentions his name, and says, 'Oh, yes, that's the golfer, isn't it?'; and someone else says, 'Oh, no, he's the usher in our church'; and still someone else says, 'Oh, no, he's the banker down there on the corner.' Finally, after talking it over, they

come to realize that these three are all one man, but they have
known him in different relationships. Yet he is one man." Then
I would warn the students, in order to avoid needless difficulty
later, that this does not represent enough of what we would
like to say about God and we will be learning more and more
all through the years. It is an endless task, coming to understand more about God, and even at the end of life it remains a
great mystery. So never think we have explained everything
about God. And second, I would warn them that while Mr.
Smith may be a very different character in church and in the
bank and on the golf course, God is not. God acts consistently,
always.

3. *At the high-school level*

At the high-school level, I should make a deliberate, direct
approach to the doctrine of the Trinity. In a class at this age,
I would be giving reasons for believing in God, among other
things. I would give philosophical reasons, as well as the biblical
grounding of our doctrine of God. These youth need to relate
their Christian faith to everything they know in their classes
at school and everywhere else. This means having to relate the
doctrine of God to some reasons for believing in God, reasons
having to do with the scientific understanding of life and the
order of nature.

Then as far as the doctrine of the Trinity is concerned, I
would tell them something of the history of the development
of the doctrine of the Trinity, very briefly, sketching some of
its highlights. I would call their attention to the development
of that interesting word *persona* which came to be used to mean
each of the three in God—each of the three Persons as we
say crudely in English. *Persona* meant a mask which one could
put on his face to make him look like someone else. Because
masks were used in the ancient dramas to represent the different
roles that were played in a drama, the word *persona* came to
mean a role in a drama. One actor might play several roles in a
drama, and hence he would be several *personae* in one play.

Gradually the word *persona* came also to mean an individual person.

At the time when the word began to be used in the ancient Trinitarian doctrine, it was a highly ambiguous word. This was precisely the reason why it was used. It was used because the church fathers did not understand very well the relation between God as they knew him in the Old Testament and through Jesus Christ and now through their own experience of the Holy Spirit. They were groping for a word which would be rich and suggestive and meaningful but would still not be more rigid and precise than their imperfect knowledge.

One can see this especially clearly in St. Augustine's great work on the Trinity where he uses analogy after analogy in his attempts to explain this great doctrine. Finally he says that all of this is very inadequate, that he cannot explain the Trinity, and what he has written has been said, not because it was precise and accurate, but because something had to be said; it was better to do one's best than to be silent. Then he asked God to fill out his ignorance with knowledge, to forgive him for all the mistaken instruction he might have given, and to enlighten him until the day when he would know God truly as he is. Certainly I would leave this subject with a sense of the mystery which is a part of what the doctrine of the Trinity represents.

4. *With adults*

If instructing adults, I would represent and teach the doctrine of the Trinity as in the high school group. But I would also be concerned with talking about how this affects our instructing of children, our understanding of the church and its task, and the implications of all this throughout adult life.

The three chapters to follow will further interpret the doctrine of the Trinity for our times and show some of its bearing on the goals, methods, and curriculum of Christian education.

V

God the Father

MANY GENERATIONS OF CHRISTIANS HAVE DECLARED, IN THE OPEN-
ing words of the Apostles' Creed, "I believe in God the Father
Almighty, Maker of heaven and earth." This doctrine is strongly
reaffirmed in the principal Christian creeds written in our
times.

Thus, the Korean Creed opens with the words, "We believe
in the one God, Maker and Ruler of all things, Father of all
men; the source of all goodness and beauty, all truth and love."
In another widely used creed, formulated by the late Edwin
Lewis, the minister and people repeat together, "We believe
in God the Father, infinite in wisdom, power and love, whose
mercy is over all His works, and whose will is ever directed to
His children's good." [1]

A. Meaning of the Fatherhood of God

1. *God the creator and sustainer of all things*

When we say "Our Father," we are expressing our Christian
belief that we and all things of our world have the source and
ground of existence in God. "In the beginning God" was at
work creating the universe. Everything else is a recent arrival
as compared with him. We and all things depend absolutely
on him.

To him belongs all our gratitude for past and present goods.
In him is all our hope for the future.

---

[1] All three creeds from which quotations are here made may be found in
their entirety in *The Book of Worship for Church and Home* (Nashville: The
Methodist Publishing House, 1944), pp. 138-40, and in *The Methodist Hymnal*
(Nashville: The Methodist Publishing House, 1939) p. 512.

We are prone to stand in awe of wealth, fame, and earthly power. But the largest human fortune is only a temporary holding of tinsel as compared with God's permanent possession of all the treasures of sky, earth, sea, sun, planets, constellations, and galaxies. The greatest human fame is only the momentary sparkle of a particle of dust in the sunlight as compared with him whose glory the heavens declare. As for power, all that is held by all mankind together is but a minute portion of that bit of his power which God has entrusted to his creatures on this planet earth.

Only God is God. There are many objects of human fear or reverence. But God is the one whom we should both fear and revere. For in him are finally determined all the issues of death and life.

2. *We were made for a divine purpose*

When we say that God is our Father, we mean also that we were created with a purpose. Man is not a cosmic accident. Neither is he a mere brute with an overdeveloped cranium. No more is he a mere system of levers and cords operated by an extraordinarily complicated control box in the skull. Human life began by the creative act of God. He made us for a purpose.

However hard he may try, man cannot content himself with being a healthy animal or an efficient automatic machine. The fulfillment of his biological impulses alone does not satisfy him. There is within him a deep yearning for some larger and more coherent realization of meaning. He wants not only to live in the world but to understand it. He wants not only to enjoy life but somehow to picture its beauty and to share it with others. He is always setting for himself ideals and then trying to reach them. Often the ideals are exceedingly unworthy and when they are, their realization leaves him still dissatisfied. But ideals he will have. As long as they are out of harmony with the purpose of God they will soon come into conflict with each other and with the realities of human nature. Only in the path which God himself planned for us can we find

both rich meaning and peace. We are made in the likeness of
God our Father and only so far as this likeness is freed from the
overlay of sin and brought to pure completeness can we feel
that we are truly ourselves.

3. *God is lawgiver and judge*

As creator-father, God laid down the laws for all his creatures.
The causal laws which the scientists discover are the laws of
God's orderly government of the world. All nature is subject
to them, testifying at every moment to the sovereignty of one
God over all.

God has chosen that human beings should be no puppets
compelled to do his bidding, but the children of his fatherly
wisdom and love. As his children we are given freedom in responsibility to obey the moral laws to which he has commanded
us to be subject. We can disobey him, but when we do, we
must face the consequences which are his painful judgments
upon us. These punishments occur in the personal fear, sorrow, strife, and emptiness of individuals; in the conflict and
destruction of races, classes, and nations, and in the judgments
we can expect after death. God is our holy judge.

4. *Our human brotherhood*

A fourth meaning of our statement that God is our Father
is that all men and women are our brothers and sisters.

In recent theological discussion there have been many con-
temptuous remarks made about the doctrine of the Fatherhood
of God and the brotherhood of man. It is true that these two
articles would constitute a highly inadequate creed. It is also
true that they are sound and important affirmations.

People who parrot the common notion that these are simply
the superficial ideas of a recent liberalism must not have read
their Bibles with very great care. That Jesus' favorite name for
God was Father and that he spoke of him as "your Father" as
well as "my Father" and that he taught us to pray calling him
"Our Father" can scarcely be doubted. As for the brotherhood,
the terms brother and sister are often used by biblical writers

in their specific family sense, referring to blood relatives, and likewise are often used concerning the intimate community of faith. On the other hand, it has been recognized by the church through the centuries that the parable of the prodigal son is also the parable of the elder brother.

This parable is eloquent proclamation that anyone who is to be a true son of his Father in heaven must also be a faithful brother to his fellow man on earth. He who will not forgive his repentant, wayward brother cannot be in the presence of the Father, for the Father has received the wayward brother into his own love and only those who are willing to share this reconciliation can now be with the Father.

All who do share the Father's love for his children—even the most unlovely and wayward ones—must participate in his ministry to them. When Jesus quoted and universalized the Old Testament commandment, "You shall love your neighbor as yourself" (Matt. 22:39; Luke 10:29-37), he did not make an exception of neighbors who were faithless and unworthy. Jesus clearly taught that he regarded all men, down to the least as his brothers and he told how "the Son of man," in the day of his glory would say to those who have tenderly ministered to the needy, "Truly, I say to you, as you did it to one of the least of these my brethren, you did it to me" (Matt. 25:31-40). If our Lord calls the least of men his "brethren," may we do less?

5. *This is God's world*

A fifth implication of our belief that God is our Father is that this is God's world. If this be true, then the natural is sacred. We must end for all time the notion that the common life of daily work, play, and rest is something merely natural and therefore lacking in sacredness. "The earth is the Lord's and the fulness thereof, the world and those who dwell therein." (Ps. 24:1.)

This being true, we, under God, are stewards of life and of all natural resources. Whatever needlessly impoverishes or endangers my life and strength I have no right to employ, for I am steward of this bodily temple which God has made. Like-

wise, as a good steward under God, I must use the natural resources—lumber, oil, fertile soil—around me with humility and
reverent responsibility as a good steward under God. What this
principle has to say concerning the use of vast portions of the
natural resources which we employ as preparation for the
wholesale destruction of the life given us is not hard to see.

Since this is God's world, the study of the natural order is
properly undertaken as a religious activity with heart sensitive
to God's self-disclosures in that order. Too often all studies of
the sciences and human history are left unrelated to the teachings of our faith and so condemned to a barren secularism.

Where, in a pluralistic society, public schools are wisely
forbidden to engage in religious instruction, a special responsibility is thus placed on church schools to make clear that this is
not because the fields of study in public schools are apart from
God, but that, on the contrary, these fields cannot be properly
and fully understood apart from him.

6. Instruction in natural theology

Because God is creator of the world and of ourselves, we can
find both within human nature and within the world around us
signs of him.

> The heavens are telling the glory of God;
>   and the firmament proclaims his handiwork.
> Day to day pours forth speech,
>   and night to night declares knowledge.
> There is no speech, nor are there words;
>   their voice is not heard;
> Yet their voice goes out through all the earth,
>   and their words to the end of the world. (Ps. 19:1-4.)

St. Paul states this truth less poetically, but with equal clarity
when he says, "Ever since the creation of the world his in-
visible nature, namely, his eternal power and deity, has been
clearly perceived in the things that have been made." (Rom.
1:20.) Again, speaking of the disclosures of God within the

human spirit, even among men who know neither Christ nor the Old Testament, Paul writes:

When Gentiles who have not the law do by nature what the law requires, they are a law to themselves, even though they do not have the law. They show that what the law requires is written on their hearts, while their conscience also bears witness and their conflicting thoughts accuse or perhaps excuse them on that day when, according to my gospel, God judges the secrets of men by Christ Jesus. (Rom. 2:14-16.)

Are we, then, offering philosophy or natural theology as substitute for the gospel? By no means. What we see dimly portrayed in nature we see made gloriously clear in Jesus. The law written in human conscience, but often confusedly and inconsistently understood, we find both taught explicitly and fulfilled concretely in Jesus Christ. The estrangement from God which our sinful violation of the moral law has caused, God's mercy given to us in Christ has overcome and so offered to us reconciliation.

When we have the gospel, why, then, give time to natural theology? It is needed for building bridges of communication to many whose thought patterns have been formed in the secular world of science and social studies and who see no place for God until we point out signs of him in the world with which they are familiar. Also, natural theology is needed to pull together the worlds of us all, living as every Christian must, both in the world of the gospel and in the world of the secular culture which surrounds us.

B. Special Significance for Christian Education

Besides contributing to the substance of the specific Christian message taught, this doctrine that God is our Father has other important significance for Christian education.

1. *The pupil seen as child of God*

The Fatherhood of God means that our approach to the student is to a son or daughter of God. However dull, saucy, or irritating he or she may happen to be, the child is to be approached with respect, sensitiveness, and expectancy. Christian instruction of the child is not the effort to raise a being that is essentially an over-developed animal into a child of God. Our task would be utterly hopeless if this were its nature. Rather, our task is to release the potential with which God has endowed the child. Christian education is not so much putting something into the child as it is a leading the child out into larger fulfillment of his being as God intended.

This does not mean that we suppose the child to be "naturally good." Human nature as it actually is, even in a child, is deeply injured and scarred by sin.

It does mean that under all the evident sin and perversity there is the God-given dissatisfaction and emptiness which makes the individual restless until he finds rest in God.[2] As the teacher brings the message prayerfully and wisely, he may always hope for the child to come out to meet him, for the faithful Christian teacher has what the child most needs. Many times the hope is fulfilled.

2. *Drawing near to all people*

Secondly, our teaching of the Christian faith must be in such a mood as to draw ourselves and our pupils nearer to each other and to non-Christian people. Exclusive separation of races or classes cannot be accepted as Christian. Frequently in the history of the church and especially in recent times there has been a strong tendency to teach Christian doctrine in a way which excludes and even belittles the people of non-Christian religions. Whatever is error and sin we are obligated, of course, to oppose no matter whether it be in ourselves or in others. However, the people who live under the sway of strange ideas, even wretchedly false ideas, are nevertheless to be approached with affection, appreciation, and concern. They, too, have been created by God and in them are to be seen the signs

[2] Cf. the opening words of Augustine's *Confessions*.

of his handiwork. Christian faith, if it be truly Christian, is full of generous love, and, therefore, will not wall us in but will release us for broader and freer appreciation of all that is truly human.

In this connection it may be worthwhile for us to observe that the Christian faith itself has drawn deeply on treasures that have come through the channels of non-Christian cultures and religions. The profound obligation which we have to the Jew should be evident to anyone who has seriously studied the Bible. The Jew had received much from Egyptians, Canaanites, and Babylonians. The careful student of the New Testament discovers that there is also here much of indebtedness to Hellenistic culture, including the Greek language in which the New Testament was originally written and also contributions from other sources such as the mystery religions of the East. In the centuries following New Testament times, the contributions of Greek civilization continued to be very large indeed. The creeds of the church were formulated largely under Greek influence. If this tended to give them a kind of esoteric flavor which sometimes repels us with its obscurity and rigidity, it nevertheless gave to Christian doctrine a structure which enabled it to persist and endure in the midst of frightful opposition and varied dissipating forces. It would require too long a digression to acknowledge the contributions of Roman law, of northern European civilization, and more recent contributions from the various nations of the world.

We can, however, speak of some suggestions from far afield to which we ought to be sensitive today. The spirituality and trust in soul force and the reconciling power of love shown by that great Hindu leader, Mohandas K. Gandhi, were undoubtedly influenced deeply by Christian teaching. On the other hand, passing through the heart and mind of Gandhi, such teaching returned with a practical relevance and profound power which have seldom, if ever, been equaled within an avowedly Christian civilization.

This fact is viewed with embarrassment by many Christians.

Instead, we ought to welcome it and appreciate with generous gratitude the contribution which Hinduism has thus made to us. For us Christ is Lord and all that is contrary to his teaching and spirit must go. On the other hand, all the treasures which are in accord with his spirit may justly be welcomed. Let us thank God that he has made us, as Christians, heirs to such rich treasure from the various cultures and even the various religions of the world.

3. *The message broader than the gospel*

Attention must be paid to "that other book of God." If God is truly the Father Almighty, maker of heaven and earth then we must look carefully at heaven and earth to learn what we can.

We do well to help young children associate the beauty, order, and wonder of nature with the wisdom and love of the Creator. At the same time we should help them to associate the destructive fury of storms and all the darker side of nature with the power, judgment, and mystery of God. Our emphasis will be on the love of God because as Christians we believe that God's basic and ultimate attitude toward us is love and also because young children especially need many assurances of love. Yet evasive sentimentality is no substitute for realistic truthfulness expressed with tender personal concern.

Our attitude toward the objectives of the physical and social sciences must be one of respect. Care must be taken to correlate scriptural teaching and our interpretations of our faith with what we know from science and from common human experience.

At this point I was prepared to make respectful but vigorous protest against one kind of statement appearing in the earlier work of my friend D. Campbell Wyckoff. Again and again Wyckoff speaks of the scope of Christian education as being, simply, "the gospel." In his work *The Gospel and Christian Education* he calls "the gospel of God's redeeming activity in Jesus Christ" the one guiding principle of Christian education "with assurance of its complete adequacy, both theologically and educationally, and with assurance of its simplicity and clarity." [3] Later in the same work Wyckoff seems to make it explicit that by "Gospel" he means no more than the specific meaning of gospel properly speaking, for he says:

The gospel provides a simple basis for the guidance of Christian education because, for all its profundity, it may be put in a simple proposition (God's redeeming work on man's behalf in Jesus Christ) and in concrete terms (as concrete as the manger, the teacher, the healer, the cross, and the empty tomb) without losing anything really essential.[4]

Similarly in the senior high document of the National Council of Churches appears this statement of objective:

The objective of Christian education is to help persons to be aware of God's self-disclosure and seeking love in Jesus Christ and to respond in faith and love—to the end that they may know who they are and what their human situation means, grow as sons of God rooted in the Christian community, live in the Spirit of God in every relationship, fulfill their common discipleship in the world, and abide in the Christian hope.[5]

Here the response with its end goal is described in broad and inclusive terms, yet the truth of God's self-disclosure to which the response is made is here again defined in the narrow terms of the single revelation of God in Jesus Christ.

I confess that I was not sure whether Wyckoff had intended thus to narrow the meaning of revelation and of the message which Christians have to proclaim. In some passages of his writing and in some remarks which he had made in discussions within National Council circles, he had seemed to envisage a

[4] *Ibid.*, p. 111. On page 112 a somewhat broader conception is hinted at but not made explicit. The narrower conception is again expressed on pp. 179-180.

[5] *The Objective of Christian Education for Senior High Young People* (New York: National Council of Churches, 1958).

larger scope. Nevertheless, the often repeated explicit and formal declaration of the scope and guiding principle of Christian education in these specific and narrow terms of the revelation in Jesus Christ have unfortunately narrowing implications.

However, with the appearance, in 1961, of Wyckoff's excellent book, *The Theory and Design of Christian Education Curriculum*,[6] my misgivings have been overcome. Although Wyckoff quotes a criticism on this point for which I shall have to accept responsibility [7] as an example of "confusion," he now makes it clear throughout his discussion of curriculum, that he conceives the scope of Christian education as much more inclusive than "the gospel" in the specific sense. He does this while still defending some of the more "Christocratic" formulas, on the ground that in all revelations of God many Christian theologians "have seen the Christ, but not always the historical Jesus." [8] On the substance of this issue, then, Wyckoff and I are happily in agreement.

It still seems to me preferable to provide for this breadth of scope in a more explicit distinction between God's revelation in Jesus Christ and his other revelations. Recent developments in theology raise suspicion about the desirability of separating "the Christ" and "the historical Jesus." Paul Tillich, for example, makes this separation the means of an almost complete denial of importance to the actual historical Jesus. The Jesus of history is the Christ of my faith, and I believe I stand here in the main stream of historic Christian teaching and experience. This is precisely the reason why the ancient church formulated the doctrine of the Trinity to preserve the full richness of God's revelation, rather than relying upon a broadened conception of Christ to include all—even though many examples of broadened Christologies can be found in both ancient and modern times.

If we are in earnest as trinitarian Christians and truly believe

[6] Philadelphia: The Westminster Press.
[7] *Ibid.*, p. 130.
[8] *Ibid.*

that God, the Father, is the maker of heaven and earth, then we ought to give more care than some theologians do to the disclosures of God as creator along with his disclosure as redeemer through Jesus Christ. These disclosures occur both in the Bible and in the world which he has made.

4. God's truth and moral law

Finally, if we take seriously our affirmation of belief in God the Father, then we must stand in awe of God's truth and of his moral law. He has made us and not we ourselves. We cannot make nor change the truth concerning our essential nature or the world in which we live. We can be in greater or less ignorance of the truth and we can come into more or less knowledge of it.

We may sometimes suppose that we can legislate our own moral law. In fact, it is a common teaching in classrooms of anthropology and sociology that there are as many systems of moral law as there are various cultures and peoples. Many an anthropologist translates the term "moral law" into the sociologically descriptive term "mores." A far-reaching result is a complete moral relativism and it is then supposed that there is no truth about what is right and what is wrong. There are only varying human interests, prejudices, and preferences. Christianity, with the various obligations which it implies, then becomes simply one set of mores which may be compared with others. There is no point in asking what is the truth and which one of the systems of mores is nearer to it; for the only truth there is about morals, if this anthropological relativism is true, is simply the true description of the systems of moral prejudices or preferences which exist in the world.

In teaching, especially from the high school level up into adulthood, we must be aware that some of our pupils are likely to be honestly convinced that there is no absolute moral law, and we need to be sensitive to the grave moral risks introduced by such beliefs.

In sharpest contrast with such relativism is the principle that

God the Father, maker of heaven and earth, is also the arbiter and judge. If God is the lawgiver and the ultimate judge, then we are subject to his law and we cannot change it. We remain ignorant of his law written into our very nature and the nature of our world by his creation at our own peril. To disregard or disobey his law is to injure ourselves and our fellows; it is not to change the truth about what is right and what is wrong. Of course different individuals and societies have conflicting ideas about moral law, but they also have about causal law. We would be foolish to suppose that because there are different opinions, there are different truths or no truth at all.

If we truly mean our frequent Christian affirmation that "we believe in God the Father Almighty, maker of heaven and earth," then, whether in teaching or in any other action, we are not free to trifle with life or to follow the whims of our own thought. Neither are we free to follow the easy way of social conformity simply because it is the popular or approved thing to do. We must constantly be in search of understanding what God's purpose for us is and what his eternal law is. Having found what is his will, we must then be determined at all cost to be obedient to it. Only by being true to the purpose of our creator can we be true to our innermost selves.

By urging the belief in the obligation to obey God's law, we are not insisting upon an external and arbitrary will imposed upon us from the outside. God is the lawgiver as he is the creator. His law is a demand of our own nature, as well as a requirement of God.

Moral autonomy in the deepest sense is the same as moral theonomy. The most worthy self-rule is also a rule of God.

To be true to my own deepest self, I must be true to the purpose of the creator who made me. I cannot obey the deepest dictates of my own personal need without obeying at the same time the will of God. This will is supremely made known to me through Jesus Christ. However, there is much of detail and of technical application which may be best understood by relating the teaching, life, death, and resurrection of Jesus to observations of human nature itself, especially as structured with precision through psychological and other scientific studies.

In the end all truth is one and all moral law is one; for God is one and he is the author of all.

VI

God the Son

WHAT DO WE MEAN WHEN WE SPEAK OF GOD THE SON? IT MAY BE important first to dispel a frequent confusion.

A. Jesus and God the Son

It is Jesus who revealed God the Son to us. In Jesus the eternal Word became flesh and lived among men. But the terms "God the Son" and "Jesus Christ" are not to be used interchangeably. God the Son is not a man. Jesus Christ was a man of the first century in ancient Palestine. In Jesus human nature and the divine nature were joined.

When Jesus prayed, a man was communing with God. Jesus emphatically and continually subordinated himself to God. The church has always maintained that God the Son was in no sense subordinate to God the Father. How could God be subordinate to God?

The relation between God the Son and God the Father is not the same as the relation between Jesus and God. God the Son and God the Father are one God disclosing himself to men in two modes of revelation and of being. Jesus is the man who is the supreme disclosure of God's nature to men.

B. Affirmations Implied by Doctrine of God the Son

1. *God is intimately concerned with human beings*

When we say we believe in God the Son, we affirm that God is not aloof from us and unconcerned with human history. We do not say this simply about Jesus, the human figure who lived in the first century; this is an affirmation about God. It did not become true of God when Jesus was born, or at any point during his life, or at his death or resurrection. It has been true from the beginning and will continue true forever. God is not aloof from us. The image that some theologians would create of a God who is aloof, impassive, unconcerned, and unrelated to us is an abstraction born of idle speculation. There is no such notion of God presented in the Scriptures nor has the church generally affirmed any such belief, whether it was speaking of God the Father, God the Son, or God the Holy Spirit. However, it is in the affirmation of God as disclosed in Jesus that we see symbolized and assured most directly and dramatically that he is intimately concerned in our human affairs.

2. *Jesus was the personal incarnation of God*

God has personally entered into history, disclosing his purpose and his love in human form. Sometimes this purpose has been barely, if at all, discernible in man's imperfection, but it was made known more fully in the greatest prophets and at last completely and clearly in Jesus Christ. The idea that God the Eternal Son, the Word, was revealed, although imperfectly, in others beside Jesus is no recent notion and no departure from ancient orthodoxy. It was affirmed emphatically in the second century by several of the church fathers and continues to be a part of the church's ancient and treasured traditions. Yet today, as in the days of Justin Martyr, Jesus is to every Christian the supreme exemplar and incarnation of the divine Word. It is in him that the Word has been made flesh and dwelt among us.

3. *Jesus Christ is our norm and judge*

The law is fulfilled in Jesus who both heightens and makes concretely personal the requirements of the law. Thus, Jesus Christ is our norm and our judge. To say that he is the judge is not to say that at some time in the present or future he changes his character from being the divine and loving redeemer to being a harsh and censorious worker of vengeful retribution upon evil doers. His sacrificial love perfected upon the cross is

itself our most exacting judge. He who judges us most severely
is also he who is our most devoted, deeply understanding, and
sacrificially loving friend.

Justice without love would be no justice, but simply censorious, arbitrary retribution. Love without justice would be
only a purposeless and unstructured sentimentality. There can
be no true and meaningful love unless real differences are defined between what is good and evil. How can I will that good
should come to another if there is not at the same time a valid
definition of what is truly good and what is truly evil? In God
love and justice are one. Justice is the structuring and formal
shape of love. Love is the motivation and personal reference of
divine justice. This profound combining of love and justice is
to be seen most of all in Jesus.

4. *We are to be like Jesus*

The goal of human life is to be Christlike. "We shall be like
him," we read in I John 3:2. The writer of the Epistle to the
Hebrews speaks of our running the race that is set before us
"looking to Jesus" (12:1-2). It has frequently been emphasized
in recent years that Jesus is no mere example for the Christian.
Certainly this is true. He discloses to us the nature of God in
addition to the rightful purpose and goal of man. However,
there is great danger that while emphasizing this disclosure of
God in Christ, we may forget the exacting demand made by his
life upon ourselves. Many who call themselves by his name are
ready to exalt him in every possible way excepting to follow
him. The cross might be elevated on every altar and shine from
every steeple and yet all the people who worship within our
churches might continue to refuse to follow the way of reconciliation by means of sacrificing love toward those who have
sinned against God and against them. Jesus said that those who
would follow him must pick up their crosses. To take up a cross
means willingly to suffer in preference to inflicting suffering;
to be humiliated in preference to humiliating others. It means
to return good for evil and love for hate. Jesus is more than

our example and goal, but he is our example and goal. It is only a farcical caricature of Christianity to suppose that people can be Christians without seeking to be like Jesus Christ.

5. *Hope of moral victory*

Human nature can be changed. How often, as men look at the stubborn social problems which we confront, do they say you cannot change human nature! Because they believe that human nature cannot be changed, they assume that racial discrimination, economic injustice, and barriers which rise between classes must always remain and that wars will never cease until that peace of death in which no one remains alive on earth. In Jesus all such excuses are torn from us.

When we suppose that in the midst of the ambiguities, hostilities, and perplexities of actual history no one could live a life of purity, we see Jesus and he compels us to revise our opinion. He pulls our defenses from us and leaves us standing guilty and defenseless before him. At the same time he gives us hope, for we see in him both what man can be within the stream of history and also the love and power which God is ready to give to us in enabling us to be like him.

Never have the hatreds of men been more intense; never have the humiliations of some men by others been more extreme; never has the hopelessness of any been more dismal than many suffered in ancient Palestine when Jesus lived. Yet we see the uncompromising purity and devotion of his deeply sympathetic and courageous life. By the grace of God which he has disclosed "we can be like him." This is a part of what we mean when we say that we believe in God the Son.

6. *Human nature dignified*

Even the most simple flesh has been sanctified by Christ's living here. No matter how wretched may be the sinner standing before us, whether a child or an adult, we are bound to view him with respect, for in Jesus Christ, our Lord God has been revealed in human form. Moreover, while he was living in human flesh, Jesus respected even the most humiliated and despised sinners. Condemned adulterers and detested tax collectors for the despotic rule of Rome clung to him with hope and he did not cast them off. The human nature which Christ has sanctified we dare not treat with disrespect.

C. Significance of Belief in God the Son for Christian Education

1. *Justification by faith*

Belief in God the Son reminds us that we are saved from sin and death, not by our own righteousness, but by the free gift of God's love in Jesus Christ accepted by our faith.

This teaching has been so prominent in Protestant history that it is sometimes called "the Protestant principle." Yet it is always in danger of being neglected in the actual practice of Christian education. For this there are understandable reasons.

Whenever Christian faith is being planted in new soil it tends to be expressed in a moralistic and even legalistic way. The ancient Christian church was rather highly legalistic in the second century, as it spread over the hitherto pagan world beyond the Jewish community. To maintain its distinctive meaning it had to be sharply defined as over against the pagan culture. The result was increasingly precise formulation of doctrine and increasingly rigorous prescriptions of Christian conduct.[1] In the present time similar tendencies can be readily seen in geographical areas where Christianity is a newcomer, as, for example, in central Africa.

In the Christian instruction of children, one is always planting the faith in new soil. With children, as with adults in newly evangelized areas, it is necessary to describe the Christian life in simple, clear terms and to stiffen moral resistance to forces threatening to compromise and destroy the distinctive meaning of the faith. Christian instruction at the age levels up through high school needs to simplify the faith and to present it more

---

[1] For ancient legalistic prescriptions of Christian conduct, see especially Clement of Alexandria, *The Instructor*.

legalistically than is permissible at the more mature levels of development.

Nevertheless, the whole faith needs to be taught at every age. The teacher must carefully avoid exemplifying or otherwise teaching self-righteous pride. At every age children are to be taught a grateful, confident dependence upon God's grace.

For the teacher this implies a candid humility. He does not, as a Christian, present himself to his pupils as a model after whom they should pattern their lives. He seeks with utmost earnestness to live the most exemplary Christian life, disciplining himself to avoid every possible occasion of stumbling. At the same time he knows that at his best he still falls far short of Christlikeness. Not seeking to defend his own righteousness, he is quick to admit mistakes or sins and point to the superiority of Christ.

He will give careful moral instruction as did Jesus and in ways commended by Jesus' example. At the same time he will continually point beyond morals to the faith in God in which all Christian morality is grounded.

From belief in justification by faith the teacher may also take comfort in his work. Often the work is discouraging and the teacher may wonder if any progress is being made. At times he makes mistakes which may upset his relations with his class and even do injury to some pupils. At such times the teacher may take comfort in the confidence that God accepts the teacher's faithful intent and by his grace uses it for his purpose. By such confidence the teacher avoids the hardening of conscience and lowering of standards, on the one hand, and on the other, the falling into discouragement and surrender of the task.

2. *Living and teaching in the spirit of Christ*

The attitude of Jesus is normative for us. Since we believe that he was the Word of God made flesh, the disclosure in human history of God the Eternal Son, the attitudes which ruled his life are guidelines for us.

In all our work of Christian education there must be ever before us the goal to live and to teach in his spirit and to assist those under our instruction to cultivate a spirit like that of Christ.

The spirit of Jesus can be described in terms of love, courage, purity, zeal for justice, and other traits of character. It is important that we make such careful observations. However, no amount of abstract definition can take the place of the concrete, living figure of Jesus as portrayed in the Gospels. To cultivate the spirit of Christ requires much time in prayerful meditation on the scriptural accounts.

3. *Every pupil a fallen child of God*

We view and treat the child not as pristine perfection, for we know as we look at Jesus that no one of our acquaintance, young or old, has actually attained to this measure of life. On the other hand, we cannot treat the child as a mere animal organism to be conditioned and trained as we would like to train it. Seeing the child in the light of Christ we view him both as inclined to sin and also as drawn to Christ's likeness.

A popular image of the child during the past several decades of Christian education has been that of a morally neutral being simply in the process of becoming either good or evil. In a sense, this image was true. The baby is certainly neither a sinner nor a righteous person and it is possible for him to become either one or the other. However, a more penetrating and realistic description of the child will present him, not as a piece of white paper on which something is to be written, but rather as a battleground on which powerful forces are already contending.

As we look at the cross of Christ we know that it exercises a great drawing power upon human nature. There is something about this sacrificial devotion of the Son of God which has unparalleled attraction for human beings. We know also that there is something offensive about it. We shrink from any such costly sacrifice. We approve it, but we should not like to be called upon to make it. This ambivalence of human attitude toward God's disclosure of his love to us shows us the better for what we are. We want to be near him and we want to be like him. We want also to have our own way and to be ourselves, free from the cost of bearing a cross or of sharing in his.

With confidence we may view the growing child, youth, and adult as a being in whom these same contending forces are in operation. We never work alone. There are forces within every human life which are working with us as we speak the word of God. These forces are the work of God himself. We may be sure, too, that there are other forces, forces of self, which are contending against us. This helps us better to understand the task which we constantly confront.

4. *The teacher as channel of God's love*

Our Christian education must be a work of redemptive love. Certainly as Christian teachers we have ideas to impart, many of them. They need to be as rigorously thought out and as precisely expressed as we are able to make them with genuine hard work. Yet the stuff of Christian instruction is not only ideas. We are seeking to reach the heart and to turn it toward God. This must be accomplished through a love which we receive from God. We turn to him for renewal and give out to those with whom we work. It is not enough that a Christian teacher love his pupils, but if he does not love them, no other quality which he may have can possibly bring him effectiveness in his task. Yet, while he loves them, he must also love God. Indeed, he must love the pupils for Christ's sake. He thus becomes a mediating link between the pupil and Christ himself. If it seems presumptuous to suggest that we may mediate between the pupil and Christ, then let me remind you of the far bolder statement of Martin Luther that every Christian should be a "Christ to his neighbor."

5. *Bringing the pupil to decision for Christ*

Since we believe in the revelation of God in Christ, it is of critical importance that we should help the pupil to come to a moment of decision to make Christ the Lord of his life.

There must be many moments of decision to yield our wills to God. In the typical growing Christian life, it is discovered again and again that there are areas of thought and will which have not yet been exposed to the grace of God much less offered to him in faithful obedience. With each such discovery there is precipitated a new crisis of decision. If growth is to continue, there must be a new decision, again and again, to give our all to him.

However, there is no gainsaying the fact that at some time it must become a guiding principle of life that all that is possessed or discovered is to be devoted to him. This one capital decision becomes a controlling principle, guiding others which are to follow. It was a grave mistake when some of our fathers supposed that every life must go downward to greater and ever more dismal depths of sin, and then, finally, be precipitated into a crisis of decisive conversion. However, it is an equally grave error to suppose that each life may quietly and smoothly grow from infancy to the grave in a gradually increasing maturity of Christian devotion. Human life grows often through crises and through decisive steps. The importance of them must not be belittled.

Most of all, we must recognize the crucial importance of the great decision to pass from being a hearer of the Christian word to one committed to uphold it and to obey it. To put the matter another way, we must regard as crucial and important the passage from receiving the benefits of Christian fellowship while not being personally committed, to a new life of firsthand decision to make Christ one's own Lord and to contribute to the fellowship by one's own offering of himself.

The need for such decision should be especially acknowledged in the instructing of children from about twelve years of age on through the teens. Yet the way should be prepared in the junior years, and even among mature adults in the church it cannot be assumed that all have made the great decision.

One of the important challenges to Christian education in our day is to find the right context and structure in which to prepare and precipitate just such critical hours of decision as may make possible the new birth of the spirit in Christ. This is not a simple matter. To prepare for a decision in depth it is necessary to convict the pupil of sin and make him feel to the core of his being the need for repentance and commitment to God. This means the fomenting of considerable emotional disturbance. Some youth who become so disturbed may not find the cure in faith. The fear of producing such disturbance has caused much of Christian education to remain at the "safer," more superficial levels. Many teachers stress the love of God and the high ideals of Christian living, while playing down all notions of God's awful judgments upon human sin. In this way the risks of producing emotional disturbance are reduced to a minimum.

Unfortunately, this concern with avoiding emotional disturbance and the upsetting of the pupil's sense of security has serious negative consequences. The reality of sin is still present, even when unmentioned and unacknowledged. The guilt is not healed and so remains to take disastrous toll. A generation singularly free from teaching and preaching about sin at church shows an apparently unprecedented rate of emotional breakdown from accumulated guilt feelings with which psychiatrists are all too familiar.

The confronting of youth with the awful realities of sin, death, and judgment is a grave responsibility, to be undertaken only with great love and much prayer. It must not be attempted by anyone who can face it lightly or enjoy it. But to avoid the necessity of such confrontation is to leave the pupils in the throes of fatal spiritual disease. Responsibly, sensitively, and carefully the judgments of God and the offer of forgiveness and new birth must be taught.

The task of Christian education is not complete, indeed it is not yet grappling with its critical problem, until it introduces the sin-burdened heart of the pupil to the healing of the Savior Jesus Christ.

VII

God the Holy Spirit

A. Doctrine of the Holy Spirit in the Bible and in the Ancient Church

1. *Beginnings in the Old Testament*

In the Old Testament there are many references to "the Spirit of God," "the Spirit of Wisdom," and, simply, "the Spirit." There are rare references to "the Holy Spirit." However, the Spirit of God is said to have come to the prophets and to have spoken to them and through them, while later, in the New Testament, the writings of these prophets are spoken of as the work of the Holy Spirit. Plainly, therefore, in the eyes of the New Testament writers the spirit referred to in the Old Testament is identical with the being called the Holy Spirit in the New.

We shall, therefore, have to say that the doctrine of the Holy Spirit clearly had its beginning in the Old Testament. Here the Spirit of God is said to have participated in the creation. This spirit spoke by Moses and the prophets. The Spirit brought to various Old Testament personalities evidences of unusual seizure by divine power. The Spirit illuminated and guided.

2. *Participating in the Incarnation*

In the New Testament the Holy Spirit is represented as having been active in the life of Jesus. In the birth story as recorded in the Gospel according to Luke, it was the Holy Spirit who miraculously brought about the conception of Jesus in the womb of his mother, Mary. Upon the first meeting of Elizabeth with Mary after the latter's conception, Elizabeth is said to have been filled with the Holy Spirit. Likewise, after the birth of John the Baptist, his father, Zechariah, was filled with the Holy Spirit and prophesied (Luke 1:67). When Jesus was taken to the temple for purification it is said that the Holy Spirit was upon Simeon and Simeon prophesied according to what had been revealed to him by the Holy Spirit (Luke 2:25-26).

When John was baptizing at the Jordan, he predicted that Jesus would baptize with the Holy Spirit (Luke 3:16). When Jesus was baptized, "the Holy Spirit descended upon him" (Luke 3:22). When Jesus went up into the wilderness to undergo temptation, it is reported to us that he was "full of the Holy Spirit" and that he was "led by the Spirit" (Luke 4:1).

All of these references seem clearly to indicate that the New Testament writers thought of the Holy Spirit as having participated in the Incarnation.

3. *The coming at Pentecost*

On the other hand, Jesus is reported to have promised that after his final departure from the earthly scene, there would come to the disciples a counselor, the Holy Spirit, who would teach them and enable them to carry out their mission. This promise has always been regarded as having been fulfilled on the day of Pentecost when the many disciples who were gathered together in Jerusalem were seized by the power of the Holy Spirit and caused great amazement among the bystanders because of their enthusiasm and the remarkable unity of their understanding, despite the human barriers of nation and language.

4. *The acts of the Holy Spirit*

Throughout the Book of Acts the Holy Spirit is at the center of attention. Indeed, the book might well be called the Book of Acts of the Holy Spirit. The apostles whose acts are described in this work are plainly regarded by the author, presumably Luke, as having been empowered for these wonderful works by the Holy Spirit.

By his power the apostles had courage to stand in the face of the greatest peril, although earlier they had all forsaken Jesus and fled in the hour of supreme testing. Likewise, it was by the power of the Holy Spirit that they were enabled to speak with remarkable boldness and persuasiveness. It was by the same power that they performed mighty acts of healing. The astonishing effectiveness of their preaching in building the church and in bringing great joy to the people was attributed to the Holy Spirit.

5. *Commemorating Jesus*

In New Testament days a major function of the Holy Spirit seems to have been thought of as the calling to mind of the life and teachings of Jesus. Indeed, the identification of the Holy Spirit with Jesus is often remarkably close. Saint Paul can speak of the spirit of God, the spirit of Christ, Christ, and the Holy Spirit all synonymously. Indeed, at one point he even says in so many words, referring plainly to Jesus, "The Lord is the Spirit" (II Cor. 3:17).

To the minds and experience of the disciples after the ascension of Jesus, his work on earth would have been at an end had not the Holy Spirit come to carry it on in their hearts and lives. Through the Holy Spirit the teaching, power, and attitudes of Jesus were not only perpetuated but became universalized without the previous restriction of time and space. The Holy Spirit was available everywhere to those who asked for this priceless gift.

6. *Teaching new truth*

Not only did the Holy Spirit recall to living memory the work of Christ; he also continued the teaching of new truth. The primitive church did not feel bound to restrict its teaching to what Jesus had explicitly taught. The Holy Spirit continued to speak and to reveal God's will.

7. *Creating the church*

The Holy Spirit is regarded as having been the founder of the church in a very real sense. Of course, Jesus is often so regarded and surely there is much to be said for this point of view. When Jesus appointed twelve apostles, certainly this number could not have been an accident. He was plainly symbolizing the establishment of a new Israel, a people of the New Covenant, a people now destined to become the redemptive community of God's purpose. There are many other signs in the Gospels that Jesus was quite purposefully intending and establishing a church. Yet the rudimentary organization which he formed among the apostles, and apparently temporarily among the seventy, appears to have broken down altogether after the Crucifixion. After the Resurrection it must have been at least partially restored, for there were many disciples together in Jerusalem on the day of Pentecost and Simon Peter preached to the assembled people as soon as the gift of the Holy Spirit was given. On the other hand, if the day of Pentecost is regarded, as is usual, as the day when the church was founded, then the Holy Spirit was the founder. It was on that date that the original, small, and loosely ordered band of Jesus' followers began that rapid expansion and organization which soon changed the whole situation in the Mediterranean Basin.

When some persons call today for a renewal of the power of the Holy Spirit in the church, one wonders how carefully they have read in the New Testament what would happen if this were actually to occur. Whenever in the New Testament there is wonder expressed at the work which the Holy Spirit was performing in the church, part of that wonder has to do with the breaking down of the barriers between race and race, nation and nation, class and class. It was the Spirit who made all one in Christ. It is ironical that some who most emphatically call for a renewal of the Holy Spirit in the church today are at the same time most stubbornly defending the walls of separation which men have created within the church, as well as in the world.

8. *An eternal mode of the Trinity*

In ancient theology the Holy Spirit was generally regarded as having come after Christ to continue his work. Yet there continued to be inconsistent references, inconsistent at least formally, to the work of the Holy Spirit in the inspiration of the Old Testament writings. The fact seems to have been that the idea of the Holy Spirit of God, speaking to men, empowering and enlightening them, was an old idea. But the experience of this inward-working God was so new and overpowering after Christ had been known among men, and this experience of the Spirit was accompanied by such new meanings as had come from the life and work of Jesus that in some contexts the Holy Spirit was spoken of as if exclusively known after Jesus' earthly ministry. However, ancient theology was quick to affirm that the Holy Spirit had really always been. The Holy Spirit, indeed, was an eternal mode or *persona* of the Holy Trinity.

While the Holy Spirit had been eternally generated in the life of God himself, he was also God revealed and immanent in individual Christian men and in faithful communities of men at particular times and places in history.

B. Importance of the Doctrine of the Holy Spirit in Present Theology

1. *God our living contemporary*

When we affirm the doctrine of the Holy Spirit, we are saying that God is our living contemporary. He is not an absentee creator who long ago left his world to go its own way, perhaps governed by certain general principles called natural or scientific laws. Neither is he merely one who made himself known to us long ago through Jesus Christ and then returned to his high heaven of heavens leaving us in wistful loneliness. God lives and will live in all times. He is our ever-present contemporary.

2. *God is immanent*

By this doctrine we also affirm that God is immanent. In a natural, but nevertheless regrettable extreme reaction against the overemphasis on divine immanence in the nineteenth century, much of theology has recently made the doctrine of divine immanence simply a name-calling device. The truth is asserted everywhere that God is transcendent. Surely he is. He is far beyond the power of our imagination, and our deepest thought cannot fully comprehend him. The distance between his sublime power and holiness and our own finite, ignorant, and sinful selves is too vast for description. At the same time, however, it has always been asserted by living faith, as it is again and again in the Bible, that God is immanent as well as transcendent. He is not only high and lifted up; he is also "not far from each one of us" (Acts 17:27). He works in the secret places of our bodies and souls. He is at work here and now, both in the individual and in the church.

3. Continuing revelation

We affirm by the doctrine of the Holy Spirit that we believe in a continuing revelation. We have yet much to learn. We need especially to learn how to apply the basic attitudes and principles of Jesus to the complexities of contemporary life which often poses for us new problems radically different from those which he faced in the historical situation which he confronted. In this present situation we not only read the pages of the Bible to learn what was said to them of old; we also think and listen sensitively and prayerfully to find what more God would say to us today. So long as we believe in the Holy Spirit we cannot escape this solemn responsibility. To embalm the teachings of the Scriptures and perhaps of the ancient councils of the church in strict and changeless formulas is to deny the doctrine of the Holy Spirit. God has not ceased to communicate with his people. We must cultivate an intellectual and spiritual hospitality to new ideas even from unlikely sources, for in excluding all such ideas out of hand, we may be excluding the very Spirit of God from revealing to us new truth. To be sure, we must discriminate carefully between truth and error. We must "test the spirits to see whether they are of God" (I John 4:1). But critical testing of new ideas is the very opposite of a rigid exclusion of all ideas which do not come to us with the certification of the past.

4. *The centrality of prayer*

The doctrine of the Holy Spirit emphasizes the centrality of prayer in the Christian life. Religion without prayer would be but a cold form or a barren theory. No amount of correct doctrine or furious activity, however well designed, can take the place of prayer. It is in prayer that the soul enters into communion with the living God. God as participant in such communion is known as the Holy Spirit.

5. *Warning against exclusive Christomonism*

When we affirm our belief in the Holy Spirit we are also implying a stand against a narrow, dogmatic Christomonism, as Henry Pitney Van Dusen has so well pointed out in his book *Spirit, Son and Father.* The Holy Spirit has spoken in many times and places and to many people other than Christians. It is an unwarranted perversion of Scripture and a denial of the Holy Spirit to say that God has in no time or place broken through the barrier between man and God, excepting in the event of Jesus Christ. Such exclusive dogmatism is simply a revelational Unitarianism of the Second Person and perverts the teaching of the Second Person at that. All trinitarian Christians should reject such narrow doctrines and insist that the whole, broad range of Christian revelation be taken into account.

6. *Salvation by grace through faith*

Finally, as we affirm the doctrine of the Holy Spirit, we are insisting that salvation is not by obedience to the law, nor is it by the affirmation of correct dogma. No theology as such can save anyone any more than can works. Salvation is given to us through faith by the grace of God. This implies a direct relation between man and God. In short, salvation is by the power of the indwelling Spirit of God—that is, the Holy Spirit. Only the Spirit of God can save us; we cannot save ourselves.

C. Special Significance for Christian Education

The doctrine of the Holy Spirit has some particular relevance to problems and issues in religious education today.

1. *The message more than the gospel*

First of all, this doctrine is a renewed warning that the message or scope of Christian education is more than "the gospel." Certainly the gospel is incomparable in its priceless worth. Yet it is a perversion of the gospel itself to present it alone. The good news of salvation in Christ came within the context of a great revelation already given through creation and through the work of many godly men in the ancient Hebrew nation. The gospel itself promised a perpetuation of the power of God that was in Christ in the Holy Spirit to follow. The Holy Spirit of God has continued to reveal his will to enlighten men and to bring power among them. All this must be included in the total scope of our message in Christian education.

2. *Religious education the teaching of relationships*

Secondly, the doctrine of the Holy Spirit helps us to answer one of the old and most persistent questions—Should Christian instruction be regarded as primarily the teaching of ideas, of attitudes, or of certain good habits? I suppose that most Christian educators would deny that it was properly conceived as any one of these three, although certainly including all in some measure. But what is religious education primarily? What is it that we are teaching? A message? Yes. Attitudes of loyalty and love? Yes. Habits of honesty, generosity, and purity? Yes. But primarily Christian education is concerned with nurturing a relationship to God. This relationship is cultivated in the context of the Christian community. As the pupil is brought into relation with God, he then finds himself in a new relation to the community of faith around him. Through this complex of relationships and the love which he receives through them, he then reaches out for a new relationship with the world—a relation of self-giving love.

Now to say that we are primarily concerned with nurturing

a relationship to God is another way of saying that we are seeking to bring the pupil into the fellowship of the Holy Spirit; or, to use another translation of the Greek word *koinonia,* to bring him into communal participation in the Holy Spirit.

3. *Faith-centered teaching*

We here approach another one of the old issues. Is our education to be idea-centered, child-centered, group-centered, life-centered, or church-centered? Every one of these competing conceptions has contributed certain positive values but each alone has also shown certain characteristic weaknesses. I would accept all as relatively important. At the same time, I would contend that the basic purpose of Christian education is to bring the pupil into participation in the gifts of the Holy Spirit. Christian education must be faith-centered, that is, centered in the faith relation to God.

Certainly the most important message in the world is to be communicated in religious education. This message consists of ideas which can be conveyed by words. It is imperative that the good news be told. We are obliged to present the good news in the context of everything else we know about God and his ways. The relations of ideas cannot be neglected in the effort to organize in orderly fashion the sequential presentation of Christian instruction. The organizing principle which is the clue to design of the curriculum in Christian education must take into account the interrelations of ideas in the message itself.

At the same time the organizing principle must surely take account of the pupil himself. He can learn well only if his own needs, ways of learning, and capacities for growth are taken fully into account. Recognition of this fact has been made especially prominent in the emphasis of those who have advocated a child-centered or life-centered curriculum.

It is also true that Christian education takes place within a context. A part of that context is the community of faith and life which we call the church. In a paper presented on November 30, 1959, to the Curriculum Study Committee of the National Council of Churches, D. Campbell Wyckoff approached

the organizing principle of curriculum in Christian education
in this way:

The following is suggested as an organizing principle that involves the dynamics or experience of individual or corporate association with and membership in the worshipping and witnessing community of persons in Christ:

The curriculum of Christian education may be organized by
planning to involve learners with all their varied needs and developing experience in the church's ongoing study, fellowship, worship,
work, witness and mission—in which they are helped to come face-
to-face with the Gospel through study of the Bible and through the
life of devotion; see the relevance of the Gospel to the understanding
of all of life—God, man, nature and history; accept the promises
and implications of the Christian faith and become committed to
membership in the worshipping and witnessing community and to
full discipleship in the world.[1]

In this statement Wyckoff was not only speaking for himself
but was also summing up progress made on this subject in
recent studies by the Curriculum Study Committee. He continued as follows:

This statement of the organizing principle of the curriculum
depends upon the concept that learning takes place through involvement. Such involvement, if it is to lead to Christian learning, defi-
nitely implies the learner's participating in a personal way in the
very life and work of the community. For curriculum purposes this
means undertaking the Christian learning task through which the
life and work of the community find expression and through which
the Christian faith and life may be known and appropriated.[2]

I believe this has been well stated. However, our affirmation
of the doctrine of the Holy Spirit requires, it seems to me, a
special emphasis on one point. The only explicit reference to

[1] D. Campbell Wyckoff, "The Design of Protestant Curriculum." Used by
permission.
[2] *Ibid.*

God in Wyckoff's statement of the organizing principle is in the part about the understanding of all of life, which understanding is to include in its scope God, man, nature, and history. To be sure there are implications concerning God in the mention of worship, in the reference to the gospel, in the mention of Bible study and the life of devotion, and later in the phrase "implications of the Christian faith." However, implication is not enough in a matter of such central importance.

It must be said explicitly and emphatically that the involvement in which alone true Christian education can take place must be primarily and above all an involvement with God himself. It is quite true that we must study the Bible; that we must try to understand all of life, including what we can know about God, man, nature, and history; but beyond all this we must be concerned with cultivating a specific personal relationship between the individual and the living God who is now present.

This leads us to yet another important implication of affirming that we believe in the Holy Spirit.

4. *Human teacher and divine teacher*

This doctrine provides us with an answer to a difficult problem concerning the role of the teacher in Christian education.

At one time it was thought that the teacher had the task of transferring certain knowledge which he had about God, Christ, and God's will for man to the pupil. Later the teacher came to be thought of more as one who sought to mold the life of the child in the likeness of Jesus Christ. The notion that the teacher is to transfer his knowledge to the pupil is subject to all the limitations of the transmissive theory of teaching and learning in general. But the idea that the teacher is to mold the pupil into the likeness of Christ is subject to the charge of presumption. Does the teacher have such sure and proper knowledge of what the likeness of Christ is that he can properly mold the life of another in accordance with his conception? Does the teacher know the particular individual, his talents, and God's specific call to him sufficiently well to be able to say exactly what this individual should be? When we regard the teacher's task in terms of an engineering or sculptural activity, we are thinking in relatively impersonal terms about the pupil himself and likewise, about God's relation to him. Meaningful as the analogy of the sculptor may be, whether as used by the ancient Plato or by a modern teacher, it simply will not do as the basic and guiding conception of the teacher's role.

Reacting against all such conceptions, we may be inclined to say that the teacher is simply to provide a climate of freedom in which the child may grow in his own individual way. As we all know, however, such a conception is likely to lead to a purposeless anarchy. Many a church school class has been reduced to a vain futility by the lack of any firm and coherent purpose on the part of the teacher in charge. When children, youth, or adults in the church school are simply released to develop in their own way, it may be the sinful propensities of their lives which become dominant rather than the elements which God would seek to nurture and which it is our task somehow to free.

A better clue is given by the New Testament. In his Letter to the Galatians, Paul said, "So that the law was our custodian until Christ came, that we might be justified by faith" (3:24). The word here translated "custodian" was translated in the King James Version as "schoolmaster." In the English Revised Version it was "tutor." None of these words is really a very satisfactory translation of the Greek word used, which is *paidagogos. Paidagogos* is, of course, the word from which is derived our English word pedagogue and likewise, pedagogy. I am wanting to suggest that actually the church school teacher, like the law, has properly the role of a pedagogue, in the ancient sense.

What is a *paidagogos?* In the first-century sense he is not the teacher who is in charge of instructing the child. Rather, as Thomas Nicol writes:

His office in the old Greek system of education was to accompany the children of the family to and from their schools, the school of the music master and the school of the physical trainer. He carried the books and instruments, the lyre and writing materials of his pupils. He was responsible for their guardianship and protection out of school hours and was expected to protect them, not only from danger to life and limb, but also from the perils of evil companionship. His pupils remained under his charge till they reached the age of puberty when they were supposed to be able to care for themselves. His status was that of a slave for the most part, but the most respected and trustworthy of the household, and care was taken that he should be correct in his language and should not tell stories to his charges likely to corrupt or deprave their morals.[3]

A *paidagogos* and likewise a person whom we call a teacher in the church school is not himself the teacher who seeks to mold the life of the pupil. Rather he is the person who takes the pupil to that Teacher.

Like the *paidagogos* of old, the present church-school staff member may well impart much information along the way. Indeed, he must do so. He must be a trustworthy guide and his life cannot be too exalted in quality for the holy task which he has to perform. The very center of his task, however, by which ultimately its success or failure must be judged, is his guiding or failing to guide the pupil into the presence, safekeeping, and instruction of the Holy Spirit himself.

For over forty years I have been a teacher in church school, in college, and in theological seminary. At present, as for several years past, I am teaching the high school class in the local church. I confess that I should feel my task both presumptuous and hopeless, were it not for the confidence that, before I have begun to teach the young people committed to my care, the Holy Spirit has already been at work with them. I should likewise think my task hopeless and also presumptuous if I did not believe firmly that while I teach, the Holy Spirit not only teaches through me but also beside me. Again and again I find

[3] Thomas Nicol, "Schoolmaster," in *Dictionary of the Apostolic Church*, ed. James Hastings (New York: Charles Scribner's Sons, 1922), II, 459. Used by permission.

that what I have failed to say the Holy Spirit has said in the private conscience and thought of the pupil. All our teaching would be quite futile if we could not depend upon the Holy Spirit to continue his work with our youth during the hours after they have left the church school and during subsequent years.

This conception of the church-school teacher's task opens the way to a less didactic and yet more profoundly purposeful work. It implies the need to lay upon the conscience and curiosity of the pupil more problems than answers. While we place in his hands the rich resources of the Scripture, of church history, and of contemporary Christian thought, we still do not pretend to have all the answers to the perplexities and problems which beset him and our present civilization. We share with him our own insights and yet we do so with humility. We seek to leave his mind eager, open, and especially sensitive to the guidance of the Holy Spirit who always reinforces and quickens in the present situation the teaching and spirit of Jesus Christ.

This work becomes especially fruitful when, in the high-school years and beyond, the church-school session and the youth activities in worship, discussion, recreation, and service are supplemented by intimate prayer groups. I am especially grateful to the high-school youth in my own class for having led my teaching out into the extension of a prayer group.

The class had not given promise of being an easy one to teach. For two years they had been without a regular teacher because they had developed a reputation for unruliness. They were extremely diverse in educational standing and included a "Kenyon-plan" senior doing work for college credit while still in high school, several college-preparatory students, others enrolled in business courses, home economics, or trade school, and one who had quit school after the tenth grade. Yet they had responded to serious instruction on the doctrinal teachings of our church and the message of the Bible.

After I had been teaching this class for less than a year, several pupils asked for a regular time during the week when those

who were most seriously interested could meet together for
devotional Bible study and prayer. I expected four or five to
respond to the invitation. Nineteen appeared. That group has
met as "the Youth Prayer Group" every week, winter and
summer, holidays and examination weeks alike, for more than
four years, though in that time there has been a total change
of personnel and the high-school graduates have formed a separate group of their own.

The prayer group has brought a radically new dimension
into the whole youth program of the church. Some of the youth
who first responded were among the more unstable young
people of the community. Some such needy persons were deliberately sought out and brought into the prayer circle by its
young members. One such young man, who had quit school,
had a long record of delinquencies and one conviction for
armed robbery before being brought into the group. He had
a record of six court convictions in the year immediately prior
to his coming and was on parole. He came sporadically, but
nevertheless was deeply moved. He still has plenty of problems,
but he has not been in court since the first night he sat in
our prayer circle; he has become a fairly faithful church attend-
ant, is holding jobs longer than ever before, and begins to have
some hope.

There had been no regular adult or youth prayer meeting
in this local church for a generation. As far as I know there had
not been anyone who had gone from the youth groups of the
church into church-related Christian service in years. Today one
young man from our original prayer group is a preministerial
college junior, one of the best church school teachers I have
ever known, and assistant pastor of his college church. One
young man from the same group is a college sophomore preparing for missionary service, a high-school senior is trying to
decide between missionary service and Christian social work,
and two college freshmen are seriously considering the ministry.
In addition, a brilliant high-school junior is studying and praying that in a career of politics he may make a genuinely Chris-

tian contribution to world peace and justice; others are aspiring to fulfill their Christian calling in various lay occupations.

Many people have asked the secret of the group's effectiveness. Actually, planned technique is almost totally lacking. The group simply exemplifies that in an expression of faith where eager hearts seek God through reverent study of the Bible and prayer, God will act. He does.

With Bibles open we read a passage of Scripture together, each person reading a verse, and we pause frequently for questions or explanations from the leader. After twenty to thirty minutes of this, we devote approximately ten minutes to earnest questioning about the meaning of one idea encountered for the lives of the youth present. Then the leader asks if there are any special requests or suggestions for prayer: perhaps a friend is sick or in trouble; perhaps there is anxiety about the international situation or some injustice in our town, for which prayers are proposed. Then we pray, for about fifteen minutes with occasional spontaneous oral prayers, but mostly in silence. Then we go home.

But wait! In silence, did I say? High-school youth praying in silence for five minutes and more at a time? Yes, and many love it! They are normal, energetic, fun-loving young people. Some drive their hot rods noisily up to a skidding stop in front of the house where we are meeting, jump out with Bibles in hand, and run into the house. Some could hardly be found at any time in their cars or at home without a radio or phonograph blaring loudly in their ears. But if we talk too long in the prayer group and they begin to fear the prayer time will be cut short, the same noisy fellows will tap their watches and whisper to me, "Time for the silence." Sometimes, perhaps, they are relieved to be able, once a week, just to be quiet with their thoughts, though they would be afraid to break the noisy custom of youth at any other time. But I think that usually they really pray and undoubtedly they sometimes find in God's word to them the answer to their deepest need.

As the Holy Spirit works in and with us in our work of Christian instruction, it is God himself who is at work. Christian education is an act of faith. It requires faith that God the Father who has made us and God who disclosed his love for us in Jesus Christ now lives and works with us as the Holy Spirit who speaks to and quickens our lives and those of our pupils. Only with his help can we hope even to begin the accomplishment of the immense task which lies before us. If we truly have faith, he will not fail us.

VIII

God's Wayward Children

CHRISTIAN TEACHING ON THE TRIUNE GOD IMPLIES VARIOUS BE-
liefs about man as well. Some such beliefs have already been
briefly stated. It is now needful that Christian teaching concerning man be brought out somewhat more fully.

A. Doctrine of Man Especially Important to Christian Education

Our understanding of what a human being is vitally affects
Christian education in three highly significant ways.

1. *Part of the Christian message*

The Bible has much to say about man. The church, throughout its history, has reflected this interest.

The Christian message concerning man is vitally needed
today. Modern men are particularly confused and concerned
about their own self-identity. The descriptions of man from the
differing standpoints of various scientific disciplines have raised
serious questions concerning the perspective from which he
may best be understood as he truly is.

Biology represents him as a mammal which has learned to walk
erect, despite a skeleton better fitted for walking on all fours.
The resultant freeing of his hands, together with a vast development of his brain, has made him capable of extraordinary
methods of survival by extension of his power through tools,
through use of power other than his own muscular strength,
and by the control and change of his environment. Psychologists
differ widely among themselves. Some keep close to biological
points of view and describe all of man's complex intellectual

and spiritual development in terms of conditioned physiological responses to stimuli. Some press the analogy of computing machines and interpret man by "cybernetics," that is, as a complex example of electronic automation. Others, influenced directly or indirectly by Sigmund Freud, describe human thought, feeling, and action as actually determined by forces beneath the threshhold of consciousness. Many other psychological views also are promoted.

Economists look upon men as producers and consumers of values. Sociologists and political scientists see them in other perspectives.

Many of these various views can be true relative to specific purposes. It is important that physicians, economists, and dieticians understand different specialized aspects of men's nature, interest, and need.

More penetrating questions remain. What am I in and for myself? What should be my real purpose in living? What am I in relation to the purpose of God? What resources and what obstructions do I offer to God's reign?

A part of the Christian message answers just such questions. The message would be incomplete without it.

2. *Determining purpose*

Since the processes of Christian education are themselves directed toward the proper fulfilling of the pupils' lives in relation to the purpose of God, the part of the message which defines such fulfillment should determine the purpose for which the message and all that happens in religious education are used.

Often this purpose is lost from view. Then religious education may be directed merely to the end of transmitting the message, of adjusting the pupil to his social environment, or to the accomplishment of other purposes defined by philosophers of education without regard to Christian belief.

3. *Affecting methods*

There are some facts about the capacities and needs of people at various ages which will be taken into account by competent educators, regardless of their religions or other doctrines of man. Teachers in Communist schools, Buddhist schools, and Christian church schools alike are compelled to give heed to the short span of attention and vocabulary limitations which characterize five-year-old children. In such matters there is much useful information to be gained by Christian educators from nonreligious writers on educational problems.

However, Christian convictions about the nature of the human pupil deeply affect the choice of methods appropriate to instructing him in the Christian faith. Indeed, these convictions should influence the methods of a Christian teacher giving instruction in any subject, even in a public school. They are particularly important to religious education because they have special relevance to the relation between the pupil and the goal of Christian faith.

B. All People Are God's Children

1. *Created by him*

Whether the teacher confronts a pupil as a frightened little child in sudden panic at separation from familiar people and surroundings or a rigidly opinionated and argumentative old man, he is dealing with a person whom God has made. God did not create only the earth in its vast spatial environment and, many hundreds of millions of years later, the first human pair; he has created, through processes which he ordained and supports, this very person now facing the teacher—and also, of course, the teacher himself.

2. *For his purpose*

God made us for a purpose. As Christians we cannot look upon any human being as merely a peculiar mammal or as a biological accident. Not only did God make this person for a purpose, as a man makes an axe or a computer; but he made this person to share his purpose as no axe nor computer can. This pupil was created to have a knowing, voluntary part in the fulfillment of God's purpose. We are neither his machines nor his domestic animals, but his children.

3. *With value and dignity*

Every human being is made sacred by being loved of God. What is of worth to God we are not to treat as being of little value.

Moreover God made each person to be himself a center of value. God not only values a man's life; he intends that the man should value his own life and consider of worth things which contribute to his well-being.

Nothing has value apart from a conscious person's desiring or treasuring it. If there is a mountain of gold on some other planet, it is of no value unless human astronauts some day enjoy it, some non-earthly persons appreciate it, or God himself approves it. An appreciating person is himself of value and also has power to create value by appreciating, producing, and sharing.

Because each person is himself a center of value, with power to increase and decrease values by his own chosen attitudes and activities, he has inherent dignity. He may not have learned to respect himself and he may not behave with dignity but he possesses dignity by reason of God's loving purpose in his creation renewed in Christ.

4. *With possibility of response to God*

Man is purposed by God to share God's values with God; God also makes possible such sharing. Some theologians contend that God has not allowed sinful man to corrupt the likeness of God in him so completely as to leave no capacity for response to him. Others say that such capacity has in fact been lost in all men, but God, in his mercy (his "prevenient grace") and even before any commitment of faith, has re-created in all the freedom to respond. Yet others say that no human being has such ability today excepting as God, by a special act of mercy, enables him on a particular occasion to respond to God's invitation. Such special gifts of his grace, they say, are given only to the chosen ones whom God has predestined for salvation.

This last view, the belief that God makes it possible for only certain chosen ones to accept his grace, seems to me contrary to much in the Scripture and in the most basic Christian understanding of God. Even in Paul's Letter to the Romans, where believers in a deterministic predestination find most apparent support for their views, there is abundant evidence to the contrary. Paul emphasizes that God gave up his son "for us all" (8:32), and God has "mercy upon all" (11:32). Although he has planned first for the Jews and then for the Gentiles to be the channels of his salvation, the branch bearing fruit for him (Rom. 7–11), the selection has not been arbitrary. If the Gentiles now cease to respond, he will turn from them and if the Jews turn to renewed response they will "be grafted back into their own olive tree" (11:17-24).

In any event, as we address the message and its invitation to the pupil, we do so in continual hope, not that we may make of him something that he is not, but that from him there will come out to meet us an eager searching for God and a hungry response to the message, the bread of life for which he has a deep affinity. Undoubtedly such searching and such response are a work of God in him—as, indeed, he is himself a work of God. Even so, it is from the depths of the mind and heart of the pupil himself that the hunger comes and as we teach we eagerly look for that.

C. All Are Enmeshed in Sin

Leaders in Christian education have reacted strongly against an earlier theological emphasis on the absolute, contemptible depravity of man. In doing so they have to some extent reflected a liberal trend at the very time when the movement for emphasis on religious education was coming to strength.

But there was a special reason why religious educators should find it hard to live with a too negative view of human nature. The communication required in instruction demands a bridge of common understanding between teacher and pupil. A teacher who starts with the assumption that a little boy or girl is a child of wrath, in whom there is nothing wholesome or good, will be hard put to it to find any basis on which to establish a relation in which communication in depth can occur. The effective teacher always finds some common standard of appeal, some agreed good, or some wholesomely acknowledged need to which persuasive approach can be made.

On the other hand, it is now widely recognized that in reaction against extremely negative views of man many theologians and religious educators have gone much too far. There is a deep, realistic wisdom in the historic Christian acknowledgment that all human beings, as we confront them in actuality, are trapped in sin.

1. *The newborn infant not a sinner but in sin*

The baby who has just been born is innocent of sin. It is both bad ethics and a blasphemy against God to say that God angrily condemns him or holds him guilty of sin committed by an ancestor of long ago. Guilt is not a substance which can be transmitted from one person to another, purely passive recipient. The child newly entered into this world has neither chosen an evil act nor willfully raised a barrier between him and God. To believe that God is now holding something against him is to take a frightfully low view of God's justice, to say nothing of his mercy or love.

While the baby is not a sinner, he has, in a terrible sense, been born into sin. He has come into a world rife with injustice, prejudice, hate, and jealous fear. Few of the people around him really live by faith in God's grace and not one does so completely. The willful self-assertion which raises barriers against God permeates the whole social atmosphere he breathes. We take great care to guard this sensitive new life from germs and even the healthiest nurse must wear a hygienic mask as she cares for him. This is good. But from the beginning he is exposed to a more deadly infection and no mask can protect him from it. Indeed, one of the surest ways to infect him most gravely is to try to isolate him from other people and especially from other children, lest he learn bad habits. The self-righteousness and individual exclusiveness of such a procedure would itself be a deadly expression of sin affecting every fiber of his soul. There is no way to protect him by walls or barriers, physical or spiritual. Walls and barriers are uniquely effective transmitters of sin.

To be born a human being is to be involved in the moral, social, and physical hazards of life in a wretchedly sinful society. No man stands outside or above this involvement. If sin is to be overcome it must be by a power more than human.

2. Righteousness requires struggle

No one lives a good life by relaxing effort and letting nature take its course. To relax moral effort is to slide into increasing selfishness, indolence, and self-indulgence. William James was not speaking as a theologian nor even as a Christian, but as an observant psychologist when he wrote that "if a brief definition of ideal or moral action were required, none could be given which would better fit the appearances than this: *It is action in the line of the greatest resistance.*" [1]

There are appalling forces loose in our world and in ourselves. Think what would be the result if all—or even any—of us were to follow the admonition of an old movie title, *Obey That Impulse!* A good life requires a high degree of self-discipline—and more than that.

3. The Fall

In Genesis a remarkable story is told, not to recount a factual history, but to illuminate certain lasting truths of human life. (Gen. 2:8-9, 15-17, 25; 3:1-24; 4:1.) The story of the Fall has been rejected by many thoughtful people because of obviously legendary elements in it, such as the talking snake, the anthropomorphic account of "God walking in the garden in the cool of the day," and the explanation of why the snake must travel flat on the ground without legs. But either to accept or reject it as

[1] *Psychology.* (New York: Henry Holt and Company, 1892), p. 444. I have quoted this passage somewhat more extensively and discussed the problem in greater detail in *A Theology of the Living Church.* Rev. ed. (New York: Harper and Row, Publishers, 1960).

factual history is to miss the point. Some people have even speculated about the kind of tree from which Adam was forbidden to eat! As if we were not told plainly that it was "the tree of the knowledge of good and evil!" Such references in the story would let any reader familiar with the ancients' way of expressing their understanding of life recognize that this is, in the finest sense, a myth. This is not to say that it is false. It is to say that its truth is not in facts about certain events long past, but in its wise interpretation of life in certain aspects perennially present.

So understood, the story of the Fall tells us how both the human race and human individuals begin life in undiscriminating innocence, but tragically overreach the bounds of their legitimate freedom in the very process of discovering it, and so grow to maturity bound in sin.

The story and the use made of it in the New Testament (e.g., in Rom. 5:12-14, 17-18) truly report that sin is profoundly social in its nature and is passed from generation to generation. It is transmitted through example, through incitement to fear and hate, through solidifying sin in institutions of organized greed and hate, and in other ways. The youth of the present generation are responsible for their sin. However, their responsibility is shared by their parents who bequeathed to them a badly infected heritage. But the parents are not alone responsible for their sin, for the responsibility is shared by *their* parents. Where and when did all this sinful mess begin? We do not know where or when, excepting that it was wherever and whenever the first man discovered his responsible freedom, but did so by overreaching its proper bounds and learned by experience "the knowledge of good and evil." We do not know his name excepting that he was man (Hebrew: *Adam*).

4. *The Fall re-enacted in every child*

The Christian educator may well be fascinated to see how well the story represents the growing to maturity of a single human being. The little child is at first innocent, knowing neither evil nor good, but simply living as made to live. One day he discovers that he has power to refuse to accept passively his mother's ministrations and he resists her. She easily outwits or overpowers him, but later he tries again. In so asserting his freedom he becomes a true individual with the power of becoming further a responsible individual. But tragically he mistakes his freedom within the prescribed limits bounded by God's laws as a boundless freedom. Resenting all restrictions of parents, teachers, the state, and God, he expresses his personal revolt in various, successive ways in early childhood, later childhood, adolescence, and, alas! even again and again in adult life.

Such re-enactment of the Fall seems to occur in every life on the road from innocence to maturity. It looks as if maturity could not be reached without falling into sin. But we must check ourselves here.

5. *This re-enactment actual but not necessary*

Only when the individual's expression of his freedom overreaches its proper bounds, does he sin. He cannot, by perpetually and meekly conforming to the wishes of others, become mature. There must be an assertion of his own will if he is to be a responsible person and not merely a conscious thing to be manipulated by others. Since God has given no other way by which responsible maturity can be reached, this is evidently in accord with his plan. But just so far as such self-assertion is necessary and inevitable it is in accord with God's will and is therefore not sin. Unfortunately, all people do actually go beyond the necessary point in their desire to find out for themselves what it is like to live beyond the limits. So they incur guilt while gaining maturity.

The New Testament tells of one exception. Jesus, we are told, was sinless. Sometimes this is interpreted to mean that he was sinless in his mature ministry. Nels Ferré maintains that the Incarnation would not have been complete had not Jesus revolted against parental authority and in this rebellion sinned, as every youth must, to move from childhood to manhood.[2] But the argument seems self-defeating. If it is required, then God purposes it and it is not sin. It is true that Jesus, in his youth, must have developed a mind of his own. Indeed, we see more than a suggestion of such development in the account of his visit in the Temple at the age of twelve, and the resultant anxiety and rebuke of his parents (Luke 2:41-48). Certainly he shows a strong independence of his parents during his mature ministry. (See Mark 3:21, 31-33.) The gospel accounts strongly suggest that some tension developed between Jesus and his parents as he claimed this manly independence. But it is one thing to say that a child must break free of emotional dependence on his parents to become mature, and that this process is likely to be painful to all concerned; it is another thing to say that this breaking free must inevitably or of necessity go beyond the limits God has purposed. It would be hard to prove that it did or did not do so in the case of Jesus. Most Christians believe, with the biblical writers, that Jesus was sinless.

D. Christian Education as Related to the Doctrine of Man

The Christian doctrine of man makes further demands on Christian education beside those already mentioned.

1. *Faithful living requires release from bondage of sin*

Establishing the relationship of faith, seen earlier as the proper goal of Christian education, is now seen to require the overcoming of obstacles raised by sin. The child or youth may move by almost imperceptible degrees from early innocence to Christian maturity. But closer examination will show that at various stages it was necessary to repent of sin and be forgiven.

Our teaching task includes not only imparting of knowledge and inciting of that whole commitment which is faith, but also the negative task of combating sin. This will include a warning of the deadly perils of sin, exhibiting God's offered cure of for-

[2] *The Sun and the Umbrella* (New York: Harper & Row, Publishers, 1953).

giveness and grace, and leading in prayers of confession by the teacher. Skill and wisdom are required to be concrete and realistic, not abstract and indefinite, while avoiding betrayal of trust, injury to sensitive children, or making sin morbidly attractive.

Sin is not overcome by direct attack upon it but by the power of God's love. Although it is necessary to declare the judgments of God and warn of specific evils, the major emphasis of Christian instruction must be, by a wide margin, on God and the life of obedient faith.

2. *Respect for the pupil's dignity and freedom*

The methods and mood of the Christian teacher should be such as to respect the right of the pupil to become or be a responsible person. It is true that children must be prevented from doing serious injury to each other and that a few must not be allowed to interfere with the learning opportunity of the rest. But within broad limits the child must learn in an atmosphere of freedom. He cannot be coerced into genuine faith, though it is possible for coercion to secure outward conformity. Since the faith relationship between the individual and God and a genuine Christian love toward other human beings are the goals of Christian education, methods must be used which provide freedom for faith and love to arise and find expression. This cannot be done without allowing the possibility of rejection and hostility toward both God and men.

3. *Provision for misconduct*

The teacher is forewarned by the Christian doctrine of man that some mischief, rejection, hostility, and evil conduct are likely to be encountered in pupils or parents. This is no reason for despair, though it should occasion the careful planning of ways to overcome it. Every teacher who has any conception of the proper goals for Christian education will have many discouraging sessions and will altogether fail to reach some people with whom he is concerned. It is needful to learn the graceful accepting of rejection and in the face of it to continue the outreach of loving concerns. This is one of the many disciplines to be undergone which make teaching a great opportunity for learning.

4. *Not molding life but eliciting response*

Christian education should be conceived and practiced, not as a molding or building of the pupils' lives, but as the elicitation of their seeking for God and their responding to him with faith and love. A pupil learns little when not actively involved. Least of all can a pupil learn to make decisive commitment to God or learn better to serve him without eager effort of his own. The God-given capacity for response to God may be confidently sought out by the teacher for the goal of religious education makes this necessary. Although hostile forces will smother this capacity in many instances, the faithful teacher will be gloriously rewarded by the eager responsiveness of some pupils —even some who for a time seemed most resistant and discouraging.

IX————

The Church

A. New Interest in Study of the Church

ONE OF THE MOST CONSPICUOUS CHARACTERISTICS OF RECENT
theology is the great amount of writing and discussion concerning the church.

1. *Long earlier neglect*

Until recently most Protestants had given very little thought
to the nature of the church. Most theological books gave little
place to discussing the church and some gave none at all. Some
Protestant writing and speech on the subject was mostly negative, consisting principally of rejection of Roman Catholic
claims which seem to identify that one church organization
with the kingdom of God.

2. *Recent studies*

In the last thirty years a great change has occurred. Books,
articles, and conferences in a steady and swelling stream have
been focused on the church, until it has become one of the
most prominent topics of theological conversation. Indeed, at
times, recently, the church has seemed so preoccupied with self-
examination that special effort has been required to direct its
attention away from itself and toward its Lord and to its task
in the world. However, there have been many reasons, most
of them sound reasons, for this renewal of interest in the serious
study of the church. Since they are also reasons why a Christian

teacher should share this interest now, it will be worthwhile to speak of them.

B. Reasons for Such Interest

1. *The ecumenical movement*

Most churches are now in much closer communication with each other than ever before since their various foundings. In local and state councils of churches, the National Council, and the World Council, churchmen encounter many kinds of churches with radically different priorities of purpose, various forms of organization, and different relations to their cultural environment. Such encounter leads naturally to the question which is right, or at least, which is better.

Moreover, many churches have recently been involved in official conversations with others, searching for a sound basis for church union. Such conversations inevitably give rise to notice of likenesses and differences and to questions regarding the proper or best forms of church structure, faith, and work.

In ecumenical relations churches which had not been devoting much attention to defining their own nature found themselves confronting churchmen of some very self-conscious communions. According to the definitions of Eastern Orthodox or Anglo-Catholic churchmen, most of the churches were ruled out as not being real churches at all. For sheer self-defense, representatives of the others found it necessary to study the theory and history of ecclesiology.

2. *Adoption of former church functions by other associations*

In the present century many functions which in former times were served by American churches have been taken on by a wide variety of benevolent associations. The Y.M.C.A., Y.W.C.A., various welfare agencies, boys' and girls' clubs, civic clubs, and many other organizations now render a wide variety of services which once depended on the church. This change has raised serious questions about the proper domain of the church.

3. *Simultaneous increase in church activities*

Paradoxically, while other organizations were taking on these functions, the scope of church activity actually widened. More elaborate and time-consuming methods of doing things, as well as the assumption of new tasks, leave many a minister so distracted by the variety of his responsibilities that he has difficulty defining his essential task.

As the pastor administers a church "program" with its endless round of committee meetings, devotes many hours per week to time-consuming counseling, calls on the sick and bereaved, solicits newcomers for their church membership, addresses luncheon clubs, prepares sermons, fights for time to study and pray for the enrichment of his personal resources, teaches special classes, and gives his support to good social causes, he is often driven to ask where, in all this, is the heart of his ministry. How, he may wonder, did his commitment to preach the gospel get him into all these activities? Such questions lead inevitably to the question, What, precisely, is the church? Until that is answered, one cannot properly weigh the priorities among various church activities.

4. *Claims of Christian living outside the church*

Many people who are not attendants or members of any church nevertheless regard themselves as Christians. Some of them regard the church as mostly a waste of time. Others think it a good influence, but find their own work and associations outside the church personally satisfying. In various forms, great numbers of Americans subscribe to the view expressed in the common statement, "I can be as good a Christian outside the church as inside."

Such a challenge makes it impossible to assume easily the traditional inseparable connection of church and Christian faith. With new urgency the serious Christian must seek to know precisely what is the relation between Christianity and the church.

5. *Struggle of church, state, and culture*

We live in a period of strong and still rising nationalism. Regardless of ideology, nation-states throughout the world are expanding their functions and their claims on their citizens. At some point in such a process, the church must help her people draw a line and say to the state, "Thus far and no farther." Otherwise the state usurps the place of God in asserting absolute claims on the individual's loyalty and obedience.

Some churches, notably the Roman Catholic, have long sought to resolve such problems by making the state subservient to the particular church. This raises serious problems for all whose loyalty is formed in other churches, in other religions, or in none. It perplexes, indeed, many thoughtful members of the very churches which gain dominance. There are thoughtful Roman Catholics who believe that the church loses some of her own spiritual purity and power when she seeks to use the power of the state for her own purposes.

Not only in relations with the state, but also in interaction with the surrounding culture, the church is pressed to define her own limits, authority, and sphere of responsibility. The church is obviously a part of society. The church shares the language, economic circumstances, and many social concerns with much of the cultural environment. At the same time, the church has, in many of the highest hours, addressed to society a highly critical, sovereign word, "Thus saith the Lord." Such a word has been addressed to many a people on many occasions in our time.

At such prophetic hours many persons, inside and outside the church, complain that it has no right to speak against majority opinion. Some would be willing to have the church participate among the various influences quietly and gradually molding the culture, but resent bitterly any forthright opposition to prevailing customs and ideas. At such times the comforting pastoral care of the church may be in sharp tension with its prophetic task.

For all such times the church needs to know clearly what is

its true nature, what is its task, and what is the true secret of its power when it has power.

C. Relevance to Christian Education

1. *Christian education a work of the church*

Among the reasons why a Christian educator needs to know clearly the nature and task of the church, an especially obvious one is that Christian education is carried on by the church. Many questions concerning the proper tasks and limits of Christian education are basically questions about the nature of the church.

2. *The church as the setting for Christian education*

Christian instruction does not go on in a social vacuum. To be effective it requires as an environment a particular kind of community, namely a true Christian church. Every church school teacher who has worked in a variety of churches knows how differently the spiritual climate of churches can affect the work of religious instruction. A church with highly developed spiritual strength and integrity can serve as a highly advantageous setting for a church school. On the other hand, a church with diffused and uncertain interests, working at cross purposes within itself, and producing a confused, ambiguous image in the community, will find it difficult to sustain a strong and effective program of religious education. For the sake of its work of Christian nurture a church needs to know its own essential nature and seek to be true to its central purpose. In order to understand the forces with which and against which he must work, the Christian educator needs to know what the true church is and measure his own church against that understanding.

3. *Christian education as builder of the church*

The church is, to a large extent, the product of the religious instruction received by its members. Whether it is true or false to its mission in the world depends largely on the preparation given its people in their Christian nurture. The Christian educator is not only an agent of the church; he is also a builder of the church. As he prepares the pupil for participation in the life of the church, the teacher needs to know what such participation truly means. This requires that he know the true nature of the church itself.

D. Origins

The full understanding of any institution is strengthened by knowledge of its origin and development. However, this is uniquely true of the church. For in its worship and preaching, instruction and testimony, the church is continually pointing back in history to Jesus Christ whom it acknowledges as Lord and without whose life and work the church would not have come into existence. Without the record, or at least the memory, of its own origin, the church could not be the church of Jesus Christ.

1. *Jesus as founder of the church*

Jesus may never have spoken explicitly of the church as such. Among the Gospels only Matthew reports any such usage. Of the two passages in Matthew in which the word occurs, one (Matt. 18:15-18) seems clearly to read back into Jesus' language an idea appropriate only at a later time. Describing the proper way in which a personal dispute should be handled by members of an organized church, this passage presupposes a condition which could not have existed in the days of Jesus, though it could have been present by the time the Gospel was written. The other passage (Matt. 16:15-19) also pertains to church discipline and its genuineness as Jesus' word is suspect, especially in view of the fact that the parallel passages in the other Gospels (Mark 8:27-30; Luke 9:18-21) do not report any reference to the church. Moreover, Luke, who like Mark and John never refers to the church in the Gospel, shows that this is not due to his personal preference not to use the word; for he uses it more than twenty times in the Book of Acts.

However, it appears that Jesus did deliberately plan the formation of a new religious community. All the Gospels tell of his gathering around himself a group of disciples for disciplined instruction and supervised work. Such activity is the work of a man self-consciously forming an ongoing organization, however simple in structure it may appear at the beginning. Moreover, it is especially significant that each of the four Gospels emphasizes that there were in this special inner circle twelve disciples, no more and no less. Every one of the Gospels at times refers to them simply as "the twelve," and Paul also does on one important occasion (I Cor. 15:5). That the disciples understood the number to be highly significant is shown by their action after Judas' defection. Despite the fact that no one who had been personally instructed with the other eleven by Jesus could take the place of Judas, they proceeded to select another to fill out the important number (Acts 1:21-26). To be sure, they took care that he should be someone who had been a follower of Jesus throughout his ministry, but it is made quite clear that he was not the only one who fulfilled this condition. Apparently there were two candidates who, as far as they could discern, would have equal claim to the vacancy. But they chose one, and only one, in order that there might again be exactly twelve.

Why twelve? Jesus was a Jew and all his disciples were Jews. Not one of such a company could be in doubt that here a new Israel was being formed, a new people of God, a people of the New Covenant. If Jesus foresaw, he could not have approved many forms and purposes that were to characterize churches called by his name. Yet he did deliberately form a new community based, not on a common ancestry in the lineage of the twelve sons of Jacob, but on a common discipleship in the spiritual lineage of twelve men who shared his ministry.

2. *Pentecost*

The church is usually regarded as having been born on the day of Pentecost in the events described in the second chapter of Acts. This idea can be accepted only with some reservations. As we have observed, Jesus himself had begun formation of the church. Moreover, the apostles are reported to have been meeting together, mending their broken ranks, and awaiting further empowering from God before launching out in the work Jesus had given them to do.

However, for the articulate message, the bold testimony, the life-transforming power, and the rapid growth of the church beginning with Pentecost, all that happened before that is seen as preparatory. If the church was conceived and nurtured in the ministry, death, and resurrection of Jesus, it was born on Pentecost. From that day its existence has been continuous and public, often stormy and sometimes in temporary decline, but unbroken and always a force with which to reckon.

3. Characteristics at Pentecost

In the same passage describing the beginning of the church by the power of the Holy Spirit, a number of acts are described which were to become parts of regular church order.

On that great occasion Peter preached a sermon of great effectiveness. Three thousand who accepted his words were baptized.

"And they devoted themselves to the apostles' teaching." (Acts 2:42.) Christian education has been an essential aspect of the church from the beginning. We read also about "the breaking of bread" (2:42, 46), which probably implies celebration of the Lord's Supper but may signify only a ceremonial meal of fellowship. Finally, we note the phrase "and the prayers" (v. 42) without which no church exists. We are told that the people attended the temple together and also met in the various homes to celebrate their new-found unity and life.

There are other characteristics of that primitive church well worth noting. They were glad. Being glad, they gave thanks and praises to God and, like glad people generally, found favor with many people around them (Acts 2:46). They shared their possessions so that the needs of all would be met (2:44-45). They were irrepressibly evangelistic and so the church grew (2:41, 47; 4:4). There were miracles performed—though solely by the apostles (2:43). The fellowship was a remarkably inclusive company embracing people of many nations, races, and classes, and both men and women (2:5, 8-11).

E. "The Body of Christ"

There are various figures used in the New Testament to describe this new fact in the world, the existing church.[1] The best known is "the body of Christ."[1]

This characterization of the church occurs in several epistles attributed to Paul. It is most developed in the twelfth chapters of Romans and I Corinthians.

1. *Many members one in Christ*

Writing to the Romans, Paul is appealing for mutual forbearance and preferment. "For as in one body we have many members," he says,

and all the members do not have the same function, so we, though many, are one body in Christ, and individually members one of another. Having gifts that differ according to the grace given to us, let us use them: if prophecy, in proportion to our faith; if service, in our serving; he who teaches, in his teaching; he who exhorts, in his exhortation; he who contributes, in liberality; he who gives aid, with zeal; he who does acts of mercy, with cheerfulness.

Let love be genuine; hate what is evil, hold fast to what is good; love one another with brotherly affection; outdo one another in showing honor. (Rom. 12:4-10.)

Similar is the context of the other passage. Writing to the church at Corinth about various causes of strife and division, he makes it clear that Christians are not all alike and are not intended to be. Yet

All these are inspired by one and the same Spirit, who apportions to each one individually as he wills.

For just as the body is one and has many members, and all the members of the body, though many, are one body, so it is with Christ. For by one Spirit we were all baptized into one body—

[1] For a detailed and careful study of these various figures, see Paul S. Minear, *Images of the Church in the New Testament* (Philadelphia: Westminster Press, 1960) .

Jews or Greeks, slaves or free—and all were made to drink of one
Spirit.

For the body does not consist of one member but of many. . . .
If one member suffers, all suffer together; if one member is honored,
all rejoice together.

Now you are the body of Christ and individually members of it.
(I Cor. 12:11-14, 26-27.)

It is important to notice that Paul does not describe the
church as some sort of half divine entity which is suspended
above us and to which we may attach ourselves. Neither is it a
priesthood, nor a building, nor an organized structure. He says
plainly, "You are the body of Christ."

But who are the people who compose the church? They are
obviously not perfect people. Paul was writing this letter precisely because there was strife and division in the church at
Corinth. Yet he makes it clear that only those who accept Christ
as their head are members of Christ's church. The church is
the fellowship of those who accept the forgiveness of God as
offered in Jesus Christ and live by faith in him. Since they have
life by the forgiveness of God, they should also be quick to forgive one another. The church is a community of forgiveness.

2. *Bound by love*

It is no accident that Paul's longest and most thorough discussion of the church as the body of Christ (I Cor. 12) is
followed immediately by his great hymn in praise of love
(I Cor. 13); for it is love which binds the members of the
church together and makes the many one body. Love is born
of faith; it comes from God. But love is the essential nature of
the bond which holds all together.

If we would understand the nature and mission of the church
we must understand the meaning of love in the New Testament.
Love is such a common word and various kinds of love are so
common in experience that everyone supposes that he knows
what it is. But careful reading soon shows that the love spoken
of in the New Testament is something special and far different

from the emotions and attitudes which usually go by that name.

The heart of the gospel is this: "God shows his love for us in that while we were yet sinners Christ died for us" (Rom. 5:8). The first and greatest commandment, said Jesus, is the command to "love the Lord your God with all your heart, and with all your soul, and with all your mind, and with all your strength" (Mark 12:28-30). The second greatest, which Jesus placed with the first, is "You shall love your neighbor as yourself" (Mark 12:31).

This love is obviously not admiration nor approval. God loves sinners and certainly he does not admire nor approve them. Admiration or approval may accompany love, but love itself is neither of these. It is not pity. God pities his children, but when we are commanded to love God we are not enjoined to pity him!

Albert Schweitzer has stirred many with his doctrine of reverence for life. Such reverence is, indeed, ennobling and worthy of praise. Jonathan Edwards went even further, with his principle of reverence, not for all living things only, but for all being whether living or not; even the hills, the sea and the sky, he thought, were worthy of reverence. But exalting as is any such reverence for life or for being, it is not love in the New Testament sense. The love of which the New Testament speaks has to do, quite specifically, with God and his human children.

Some, like Joseph Butler, have thought that love was a general good will, an active desire for everyone to have a good life. Even John Wesley's writing sometimes reflects this interpretation. But Wesley's experience and action disclose something far more radical, passionate, and revolutionary in force than this. Besides, it would make no sense to love God in this way. We could hardly be exercised to act for the enrichment of God's life.

The most famous interpretation of Christian love in the history of the church is that of Augustine. Love as understood by Augustine is called *caritas*, using the Latin word which he employed. He thought that the worthiness of love must always depend on the worthiness of its object. Hence the highest love is love toward God. Only such love, he maintained, is worthy to be called Christian love. Then what of the command to love your neighbor? It is clear, thought Augustine, that when the Christian loves his neighbor with true *caritas* love, he is loving God in the neighbor. Since the neighbor bears the image of God he is worthy to be loved. When God himself loves a sinner, God is loving himself, the true perfection of all good in the sinner. It is true that the sinner does not show forth that perfection. Yet even when man has sinned and blackened the image of God in him, he is still God's handiwork and he still belongs to God. God loves himself in the sinner by placing in the sinner his own love for his own divine perfection.

Yet this is strained. It lacks the simple directness and power of Jesus' teaching. The father of the prodigal son loves the wayward son for the son's own sake.

Anders Nygren has stirred many readers by his great historical and systematic study of *Agape* and *Eros,* New Testament love and the lofty, aspiring love praised by the Greek philosophers such as Plato. While love, to Plato, is aspiration for the good, beautiful, and true, Christian love is not seeking to gain anything, not even virtue or God. Christian love, insists Nygren, is an utter giving of self for the sake of the other. God gives to us life and new life, not to gain anything for himself, but simply out of the fullness of his own bounty. Only by receiving such love from him, Nygren teaches, are we enabled to love others in this free, utterly self-forgetful way. Even to aspire to such love is to fall back into the Greek *eros.* The Christian *agape* cannot be gained by aspiring to it, but only by receiving in gratitude the love of God.

Nygren has, without doubt, faithfully portrayed some important aspects of love in the New Testament sense. We are enabled to love only by God's prior love to us. Christian love is given regardless of whether there appears to be any worthiness to be loved in the life of the needy person. The unlovely may elicit a special intensity of Christian love through their very need of love. Christian love needs no reward save the loving.

Yet, with all its truth, Nygren's understanding still falls short of New Testament teaching. If love is as he describes it, how shall we love God? On this question he becomes hesitant and unclear. We cannot, of course, turn to God with the desire to bring some benefit to God and with no hope of benefit to ourselves! We know full well that infinite resources are his and that in any relationship between us we must be the gainers. Besides, would any of us want to be loved as Nygren says Christians should love us? Do I want another to love me with the desire to give to me but neither hope nor desire to receive anything from the relationship? I confess that only in certain desperate crises should I care to receive such condescending, one-sided ministration from any human being. I should always prefer to be loved by someone who sees in me some possibility of a personal contribution to our relationship.

3. Koinonia love

Nygren has missed what has strangely been overlooked in nearly all theological thought about New Testament love—even when such love was being manifested in great power and beauty. The meaning of *agape,* or Christian love, is illuminated in another great New Testament reality represented by a rich, meaningful Greek word, *koinonia. Koinonia* is variously translated as participation, fellowship, communion, sharing. It is, in general, a holding something in common.

Theologians have usually defined love in terms of the quality of an object or the quality of the subject's own attitude. The person loving and the person loved have been viewed as absolutely separate individuals with their own altogether individual values. The New Testament is full of evidence and rejoicing that just such individual separation is broken down when people have faith in Christ and receive the blessings of the Holy Spirit. Even the I-thou relation is transcended in a joyously discovered "we," and hitherto separated individuals become members of one body.

There is some suggestion of this in all worthy friendship and love, even without the special dimension of depth provided in the New Testament setting. If you love another person in your household, then when you have an experience which you value, you will have a strong impulse to share it so that the two of you can enjoy it together. It may be a funny incident, a beautiful sunset, a prized honor, or a treasured gift. Whatever you value, you will want to share its enjoyment with your friend.

Christian love is like that, excepting that the treasure is so wonderful that it fills its recipient with yearning to share it with *anyone,* however unlovely. The treasure is the love of God as revealed in Jesus Christ. Having received the full impact of this wonderful disclosure, the Christian, filled with gratitude and joy, desires to share with every neighbor the enjoyment of all God's bountiful gifts. This sharing is the *koinonia,* which formed the very life of the church. It broke down every wall of separation erected by the world between races, nations, and classes of men to form one body, "the body of Christ."

In the body of Christ all the differences which the world considers so important are nothing by comparison with the lordship of Jesus Christ. The pages of the New Testament glow with joy in this discovery of inclusive fellowship in Christ. The story of Pentecost in the Acts lists the many nations represented in the primitive church. Again and again Paul glories in the fact that in Christ racial and national differences fade into insignificance. "For by one Spirit," said Paul, "we were all baptized into one body—Jews or Greeks, slaves or free—and all were made to drink of one Spirit" (I Cor. 12:13). "Here [in the Christian fellowship]," he said, "there cannot be Greek and Jew, circumcised and uncircumcised, barbarian, Scythian, slave, free man, but Christ is all, and in all" (Col. 3:11).

"You are the body of Christ" (I Cor. 12:27), so far as you live in this relation to Christ and hence to all neighbors. Any given church organization embodies the true, living church of Jesus Christ so far, and only so far, as it embodies this kind of spirit. For obviously, where the body of Christ is present, the spirit of Christ reigns and unites the hearts and lives of all.

4. *Essential to salvation*

Protestants have often attacked Roman Catholic use of St. Cyprian's famous words, "Outside the church no salvation." Actually, the trouble is not with the statement itself, but with the papal interpretation of the church.

When we are speaking of the church as the community of faith, forgiveness, and love of which Christ is the head, we can truly say that there is no salvation outside this church. That wholeness of life, free from the domination of sin and fear, which we know as salvation comes to an individual only through the living community. God acts for the salvation of individuals only through this community. Moreover, any individual who receives God's love with a grateful heart inevitably reaches out with love to share God's gifts with others. The result is membership in the living church.

The church is not an elective of the Christian life. It is essential both as means and meaning of that life.

F. The Church Today

1. *Its divisions*

The number of Christian denominations is sad evidence of our division. Denominational separation perpetuates many cultural, economic, racial, theological, and organizational disputes. Often the denominations are involved in confusing and disgraceful competition. Even when at the national or world levels two denominations are quite congenial, in the local community there is sometimes a shameful distrust and hostility between them.

Any missionary can tell how ridiculous and confusing the situation becomes when the national or social divisions in one part of the world are carried by the church into another. When Africans have to try explaining the difference between their Swedish Baptist, American Baptist, and National (American

Negro) Baptist churches, the situation would be comic were it not so tragic.

We must not ignore the positive good contributed by such divisions. Some denominations, like the Friends and the Mennonites, serve specialized purposes which more highly institutionalized churches could not meet so well. There can be a positively useful division of labor among churches.

Various forms of worship and styles of preaching appeal to people of different temperaments and types of culture. Several churches of different traditions in one community may therefore reach and serve more people than any one church which could be devised.

By the existence of several denominations, the believer is relieved from dependence on a particular one for the expression and nurture of his faith. If one church falls under dominating, ineffective, or corrupt rule, the individual can leave to enter another. This possibility is a safeguard of individual freedom. Perhaps the very existence of the possibility often gives rise to a healthy competition among the churches as they seek to provide in superior fashion for Christian nurture and expression. On the other hand, it must be conceded that the same pressures may lead to unwholesome efforts to please the crowd and to the omitting of all church discipline and all preaching of God's judgments. They may also encourage undignified and unseemly practice in order to catch popular favor and new members.

Indeed, a fearful price is paid for our many denominations. Businessmen often speak of the inefficiency and waste when several small churches compete where only one could be strong enough to provide for its own ongoing program and have money and energy to spare for the Christian mission to the world. Considering the small proportion of national or world wealth which goes into the Christian church, there is little cause for regret that what we do is needlessly expensive. But there is serious cause for lament when we waste through fruitless duplication of effort in our home communities what we would better devote to service of the world's great need.

More serious still is the confusion stirred in the world and even among church people by the babble of opposing voices which often claim the exclusive way to gospel truth and real fidelity to God. Our divisions are also symptomatic of deeper sin. Many of them show how deeply the world has invaded our church life, so that the same differences of national origin, race, economic class, and even political faction which divide the world also divide the church. Many times when it is claimed that we are divided by grave theological convictions or pious obedience to God's commands, analysis will show that these claims are barely concealing less worthy causes. Anyone who doubts this should read H. Richard Niebuhr's *The Social Sources of Denominationalism* [2] or his *The Kingdom of God in America*.[3]

Moreover, our division tragically weakens the witness of the church to the world for reconciliation and peace. When the church urges the nations to resolve their differences peacefully, its words are undermined by the obvious fact that the churches do not resolve their own differences. It is true that they do not often engage in physical combat over them, but at this point the comparison is unfair to governments because many churches can exist in the same territory, while various competing governments cannot do this. In addition, the kinds of issues which divide governments have to be resolved in some way because land and goods and other resources are limited in quantity. When there are rival claims to them, these rival claims cannot all be fulfilled. On the other hand, the primary concerns of churches are with values subject to indefinitely great parallel use and appreciation. In this time, when men must learn to resolve their differences by peaceful means or perish, it is tragic that the church has not been able to show the way to the reconciliation which it preaches to the world.

Finally, the denominational division of the church disrupts a fellowship profoundly needed. People who are together at

[2] New York: Meridian Books.
[3] New York: Harper Torchbooks.

work and who need to have their relationship at work personalized, cleansed, and sanctified by worshiping together are often kept from such experience only by their being members of different denominations. Young people who should be experiencing the cleansing and elevation of their relations at school and in the forming of friendships, some of which lead to marriage, are deprived of these blessings by denominational separation.

The disunity represented by denominationalism is only one part of the disunity with which we are afflicted. Sometimes in the same neighborhood there are churches belonging to a single denomination but representing such conflicting traditions and employing such competitive methods that they manifest the same evils apparent in denominational division. Even more serious is the provincialism which makes many a local church almost a separate entity in the thought and loyalty of its people, with scarcely any consciousness of the world church or of the world Christian mission.

Worst of all is the exclusion of fellow Christians from fellowship and the sacraments solely on grounds of race. With such practice the New Testament is in sharpest contrast. Again and again in the Acts and the epistles there is rejoicing in the interracial and international inclusiveness of the church.

In the Letter to the Ephesians, concerning dissension between Jews and Gentiles, we read:

For he is our peace, who has made us both one, and has broken down the dividing wall of hostility, by abolishing in his flesh the law of commandments and ordinances, that he might create in himself one new man in place of the two, so making peace, and might reconcile us both to God in one body through the cross, thereby bringing the hostility to an end. (Eph. 2:14-16.)

The efforts of the apostles to hold the church together in faithfulness to its one Lord were successful. Even the passionate hostilities which existed among the peoples represented in the church did not break the church of the first century into national or racial parts. Only later, when love of office, prestige, and material advantage overlaid the grateful love to Christ, did the churches fall into segments analogous to the racial, political, or cultural alignments of the world. By our own acceptance of the world's prejudiced division along racial lines, we deny the very nature and meaning of the church.

Often people in the church pray for the Holy Spirit to come in power. Many of them would not be ready for the event if it were to happen. Let them read in the Book of Acts what happened when the Holy Spirit came at Pentecost. When the Holy Spirit comes we are all—all nationalities, classes and races—made one in Christ. We need to be reminded of that, and then, with fervent hearts, to pray for the gift of the Holy Spirit.

2. *Its unity*

Tragically divided though the church is today, it is nevertheless one. The unity which exists under and through the divisions is often overlooked in a mood of impatience with our present division. This unity is of several kinds.

a) *In the purpose of God*

More important to the Christian than any empirically observable actualities is the will of God. "If God is for us, who is against us?" (Rom. 8:31.) We who draw our faith from the New Testament can hardly doubt that in the purpose of God the church is one. The very nature of the church is to be a community of reconciling faith and love. To reconcile is to bring together. Those who are reconciled and brought together are one. Every division which separates us, every attitude which makes us want to be apart from Christian brothers and sisters is sign and proof that our reconciliation is incomplete. This is not due to imperfection in God's work of reconciliation in Jesus. He has given to us his perfect love in the one perfect gift of Christ. It is our response which is halting and ambiguous.

John gives an authentic Christian testimony to the very nature of Christ when he represents him as praying for the unity of all who are now or who are to be his people (John 17:11, 20-26) :

I do not pray for these only, but also for those who are to believe in me through their word, that they may all be one; even as thou, Father, art in me, and I in thee, that they also may be in us, so that the world may believe that thou hast sent me (20-21).

Our faith is centered in the belief that, at the least, Christ, as we thus see him through the eyes of faith, represents truly the very spirit and will of God. This, then, is God's purpose, that we should "all be one." The unity of the church is an essential testimony "that the world may believe" (17:21).

The words of this great prayer seem designed to strip our excuses from us. "We really *are* one *spiritually*," we may say. "Must we actually be associated together in one organization? Is it not enough to recognize all the Christian bodies as equal, even though they be separate?" But we read:

The glory which thou hast given me I have given to them, that they may be one even as we are one, I in them and thou in me, that they may become perfectly one, so that the world may know that thou hast sent me and hast loved them even as thou hast loved me (17:22-23).

Is the glory of God which was given to Christ seen in our poor practice of unity? Are we "perfectly one"? Do we love all of Christ's other disciples, of whatever church, race, or condition with that love with which God has loved his faithful Son our Lord?

In Ephesians 4, the nature of ours and the church's calling is concisely and emphatically stated:

There is one body and one Spirit, just as you were called to the one hope that belongs to your call, one Lord, one faith, one baptism, one God and Father of us all, who is above all and through all and in all (4-6).

This essential unity of the church is described to reinforce the writer's exhortation

to lead a life worthy of the calling to which you have been called, with all lowliness and meekness, with patience, forbearing one another in love, eager to maintain the unity of the Spirit in the bond of peace (1-3).

But we differ from each other, we protest. We have different temperaments, different traditions, and different cultures. Paul has replied with unanswerable finality. We are many members, with as much variety in gifts as may be found among the functions of different parts of the human body. But differences are no fit reason for separation. Rather our differences display our need for each other that we may be made whole in one another. The many members, with their variety of gifts, were prepared by God's appointment to be one body. Difference can be acknowledged and accepted within one body if only true Christian love is there (I Cor. 12–13). Precisely such unity in freedom to be different, yet together in love, is God's purpose for us.

b) In faith

From our human side, too, there is already much of unity. God has shared his purpose with us and by his grace made us one in faith in Christ. Despite our diversity of doctrines and practices, true Christians everywhere are united by personal relationship to Christ. Two beloved friends separated by thousands of miles may sometimes be made to feel nearer to each other when a third person loved by both goes from one to the other. Much more, as I pray to God in the name of Christ my Lord, the same God, known through the same Christ, is in communion also with other Christians separated from me by all kinds of social, cultural, and doctrinal distance. The direct bonds between my neighbor and me may be weak, but we are knit together by our common allegiance to the one Christ. Indeed, if the direct bonds between members of the one church are to be strengthened until we are truly members one of another, that will be accomplished by strengthening the bonds which unite us to Christ, the head of the body.

Someone may protest that various people who are called Christians have such different conceptions of Jesus and of God that we are actually united to different beings, even though we may call them by the one name, Christ.

If Christ be only a concept in the human mind, then this is, of course, true. However, it is not by being related to concepts in our minds that we live. We are not saved by ideas, however true and good. This is not to minimize the great importance of ideas. We need to take all possible care to correct our ideas by mutual criticism, prayer, and study. Ideas point us toward or away from God. They may help us to obey or to disobey his will. But no theology can save us; only God can do that. If we have life in Christ this life comes to us from God and has been mediated to us by the real Jesus. All people of genuine Christian faith, however praiseworthy or deplorable their understanding of Jesus and of the Father, are related to the one God who is and who far transcends all opinions about him and to the one Jesus Christ through whom the Father's love is mediated to us. In this relationship to God through Christ we are one—Protestants; Roman Catholics; Eastern Orthodox; radical sect members; classes, nations, or races estranged from each other: all are, even now, one through our common faith in Christ if only we put our faith in him.

c) Many common expressions of faith

The unity which we have in Christ is supplemented by a wide, though not universal unity in many of its interpretations and expressions. Almost all of us are baptized "in the name of the Father and of the Son and of the Holy Spirit." Moreover, most of us acknowledge as valid the baptism performed in other churches; it is noteworthy that even the Roman Catholic Church makes such acknowledgment. Nearly all who confess Christ read reverently the same Bible in various languages and versions and with some minor variations in the breadth of the canon. Most of us engage in similar rites of eating bread and drinking wine consecrated in remembrance of Christ. The similarity is real and important, despite considerable differences of interpretation and despite the exclusion from the Lord's table by some churches of communicants from others.

We share very widely many other symbols of our faith, especially the cross. We agree that this life as lived in faith, by the gracious help of God, is good. Often this is taken for granted in Christendom and we might take it for granted that the positive and high appreciation of life belonged simply to our common humanity. However, this is by no means universal outside Christian circles.

d) Experienced fellowship

We are joined by many personal ties of treasured Christian fellowship across denominational lines. Most Christians in America have personal ties with members of churches other than their own. Among missionaries sent to represent Christ and the church in foreign service, such ties are generally broader and even more important. It is fortunately rare, as well as regrettable, to find a missionary who seeks to confine his personal friendship to members of his own denomination. Often when representatives of narrowly exclusive sects are found at work abroad, it is surprising and heartwarming to see the breadth and generosity of their personal associations. All these personal ties of Christian love knit together in a fellowship of actual experience a vast company of Christians reaching round the world and across every man-made barrier. Even "iron" and "bamboo" curtains have not wholly disrupted it.

e) Interchange of members and ministers

Even at official levels the barriers between denominations are far less formidable than outsiders often suppose them to be. In many an American church it can be noted that among a large group of new members at the altar many come from other denominations, varying from Roman Catholic to Southern Baptist. This is going on in every community where there is a rapidly changing population. It means that the divisions between denominations are not so absolute as many people think. The fre-

quent transfer of ministers among major Protestant denominations also serves to show how low the barriers are and to lower
them further.

For all the unity we have, we may well thank God, while still
seeking prayerfully to overcome by God's grace the divisions
which separate and weaken us.

G. The Context of Christian Education

1. *The organized church*

It is usually too obvious to be overlooked that Christian
education is carried on in the environment of a local church.
The importance of this relationship is greater than numerous
church people understand.

The effectiveness of the instruction in a church school class
depends, of course, on many things—skill and dedication of the
teacher, appropriateness and Christian fidelity of the literature,
suitability of room and furniture, audio-visual equipment, and
other factors. But the character of the church itself is one of
the most important influences. The factors already mentioned
are much affected by the Christian zeal and responsible concern
for youth which prevail in the church. In addition, the spiritual
atmosphere of the church profoundly affects directly the depth
and effectiveness of the religious education taking place within
it.

If the adults in the church consider generally that they have
advanced as far as they are going in the Christian life; and if
most of them have little Christian literature in the home and
attend no classes for further study of their faith, the negative
effects will be felt right down through the church school. When
adults are not devoting time to religious studies, young people
are likely to think that church school is "kid stuff" and so
beneath them. This attitude affects, in turn, high school and
even junior high youth.

Adults often tell a new pastor not to spend too much time
with them but to concentrate his attentions on the youth. However well-intentioned such remarks may be, they represent an

evasion of Christian responsibility. Any man or woman who is aware how great is the task of meeting the problems of the world in a mature Christian fashion will know that he or she urgently needs help.

When the laymen of a church are trying earnestly to learn and discharge their full Christian responsibilities they will develop a momentum of concerted study, serious worship, and adventuresome work which will contagiously affect younger people all the way down to the youngest children. The church school workers are not the only educators in the church. For good or ill, all the adults of the church are participants in religious education.

2. *The universal church*

The Christian educator needs to be aware also of the universal church of Jesus Christ which is found in many lands and is composed of varied denominations. Many denominational boards of education are now doing much of their curricular planning together. The resulting lessons are designed to cultivate awareness of the whole world church and loyalty to Jesus Christ, rather than a narrow sectarianism. Teachers who wish to be involved in authentic *Christian* education have a right to insist on material of this kind.

This does not mean teaching the false notion that all churches are alike or that one is as good as another. Understanding the particular world responsibilities of one's own church is important and many of them are still to be discharged mainly through denominational programs. The teachings of one's church need to be studied carefully, for loyalties which are vague and abstract are not likely to be effective. People who profess loyalty to Christianity but not to any particular church usually settle for a general religiosity too vague to be worthy of being called Christian or else they start new denominations to protest against denominations!

Rather, we should study the history, teachings, and program of our own church in the light of the New Testament and in the context of the whole church universal. The local church and the denomination rightly claim a Christian's allegiance so far, and only so far, as they are loyal to and contribute to the advance of the whole Christian cause in the world. A church which lives by attacks on all others makes the task of *Christian* education under its auspices difficult.

There are many ways in which a teacher can help make his pupils aware of the universal church. He can read publications of the Division of Christian Education, National Council of Churches and, when appropriate, use them to supplement his regular curricular literature. He can also read *The Christian Century* or other nondenominational Christian periodicals which introduce the news and thought of the Christian world. He can lead the older youth into interchurch conferences. He can take care to speak of beliefs and practices in other churches with regard for sympathetic understanding, while yet maintaining critical freedom. In all these ways and others he can help his pupils to think of themselves as Christians of the universal church, in which they are called to serve through their own particular church organization.

It is not important that the congregation use in morning worship the Apostles' Creed which includes the words, "I believe in the holy catholic church." There are advantages in using other creeds which better represent the whole round of living Christian convictions. But it is exceedingly important that we all learn to say by church policy, by personal conviction, and by inclusive Christian concern, "I believe in the holy catholic church." How else can one truly be a member of the body of Christ?

X

The Christian and the World

A. Christian Education in the World

WHILE THE FOUNTAIN AND USUAL ENVIRONMENT OF CHRISTIAN education is the church, Christian education always takes place in the world. This does not mean merely the obvious fact that this work goes on among the people of the earth; it means also that its environment is non-Christian and worldly, as well as Christian and churchly.

1. *Pupils live in the world*

The pupils, whether young or old, come to classes from activities and companions rooted in assumptions different from the convictions of Christian faith and often hostile to those convictions. Outside the church—and alas! sometimes within the association we call the church—it is generally assumed that success, good health, and pleasure are the principal goals of life.

The set of values assumed as a basis of public education in the United States is derived from the common American citizenship and not from a common faith in Christ. This is not a criticism of the public schools. Given a society of varied religious loyalties, compulsory education, and the wise constitutional provision for separation of church and state, the public schools can scarcely do otherwise. Generally, the schools teach high ideals of human brotherhood, honesty, generosity, courage, industry, and other virtues. The prevalent moral level of life in the schools is far higher than that which characterizes the community at large. Yet it is not avowedly Christian. Many Christian teachers in the public school are among the finest representatives of their faith. Their faith tends to support such genuine Christian virtues as gratitude to God, forgiving love, and confident trust in times of peril. But the very fact that in the public school classroom such virtues cannot be taught as requirements and fruits of Christian faith is confusing to the pupils. They usually do not see their teachers at worship in their various churches, but they do join with them in the rituals of American patriotism. The result is likely to be a further encouragement of that "American religiosity-in-general" which too often passes for Christianity.

Outside of the schoolroom our youth are subjected to innumerable influences representing the most vulgar and immoral elements in our society. Television and movies pour out scenes of violence, passion, and sensuous pleasure in a continual stream. Older youth teach younger children disrespect for law, for property, and for the rights of others. Public news of corruption in government, together with common observation of profitable illegal gambling and other notorious lawbreaking which is publicly disregarded, further aggravate the temptation to youthful lawlessness. When the youth engage in efforts to "make a fast buck" or seek the much touted pleasures of strong drink, illicit sex, or drugs, they are following paths well-beaten in the adult community.

There are also the "respectable vices" which pass unchallenged as admirable virtues in many American communities. These include proud and complacent self-righteousness that often takes the form of pride in neither being nor claiming to be very righteous, but feeling smugly superior to those who take their religion seriously. Then there is the hatred of Communists which commonly brings the declaration, "Once a Communist, always a Communist," and thus denies the power of Christ while at the same time disobeying the commands of love and forgiveness. All the people of the Communist-dominated countries are then commonly lumped together and regarded as the threatening enemy who is to be treated solely with distrust and hostility. This is done in total ignorance or disregard for the millions of Christians [1] behind the iron curtain who remain steadfastly faithful despite constant anti-religious propaganda, threats, and discriminating economic, educational, and political policies. Most American communities also have racial, religious, or other minorities on whom it is socially acceptable to look down and against whom various discriminations are commonly practiced. Along with all this is the common American assumption that if any Communist country attacks any political ally of the United States, we ought to unleash against the population of the attacking nation an all-out nuclear attack, even though that would incite the same kind of attack against our allies and ourselves and perhaps leave the world's population dead or, in a few generations, defective and dying.

The Christian educator needs to be aware of the confusing and often hostile world in which his pupils live and which they bring with them to the church. He must be aware of it if he is to communicate with them where they are, minister to their personal needs, and lead them out to Christ.

2. *The teacher, too, is marked by the world*

The teacher must also be aware that he is in the world and that he, too, brings it with him into the classroom. Only as he seeks continually the forgiveness and renewal of God in his own heart and mind and life, can he be fit to call others out of the world to faith in Christ.

3. *Preparation for Christian living in the world*

It is not that we would either leave the world or call others to leave it. Even if we were to hide ourselves away in monastic

---

[1] *The Christian Year Book* of 1957 estimated that there were 90 million Eastern Orthodox members in the U.S.S.R. Other estimates—probably more nearly accurate—range from 25 to 50 million. There are also reported to be 4 to 5 million Baptists, and well over one million Lutherans in that country. In some Communist-ruled countries church people constitute much larger proportions of the populations.

settlements, we should find, as so many monks and nuns have observed, that the world had also entered with us who had sought to escape it. Moreover, Christ did not call us to desert the world and leave it to its fate. He called us to go into the world and minister to its people, even the most sinful ones.

Christian education has the task of preparing the pupils to live in the world without conforming to it, ministering to its people in the spirit of Christ, and transforming the world by his power. One of the greatest rewards of teaching in Christian education is that while teaching others the teacher is himself learning better to live such a victorious life of Christian faith and service. As many teachers have learned, there is no other way of learning which can equal teaching.

B. Incarnation and Involvement

God has often been represented in speculation as distant, aloof and unconcerned with the strife and pain of the world. He has then been highly praised for being above all the perils and pains of involvement in our changing and uncertain history.

God, as Christians know him, is not such an aloof, unconcerned being. He was known to Israel as Yahweh who chose them, led them out of slavery, grieved over their waywardness and sufferings, and, in his steadfast love, promised the fulfillment of their highest hopes to those who obediently trusted in him. To the Christian, God is the Father Almighty who rules all the heavenly spheres; but he is also the Son incarnate in Jesus of Nazareth. In Jesus God offered his purpose and his love to sinful men. He took this risk. He did not hold his Spirit out of the reach of men, so they could not treat him with humiliating irreverence. He took the risk of entering history as a humble servant.

Moreover, he lost the gamble, as anyone could see. Men despised, condemned, spat upon, tortured, and killed Jesus. It was through this terrible humiliation at the hands of sinful men that God won the victory of redemption for us.

Yet there are those Christians in every age who counsel withdrawal from all the risks of involvement in the world. In order to protect the purity of Christian life some withdraw into monastic retreats where they refrain from marriage, politics, and other civic participation; and keep economic and social relations to a minimum. Others are more fearful for purity of doctrine. While participating freely in the life of the larger community, they avoid involvement in the philosophical issues which are discussed in university classrooms. Even when it seems that ideas of major concern to Christian faith are at stake (as, for example, belief in a conscious, purposive deity or in moral norms beyond the relativities of human opinion) they refuse to take sides in the arguments. Rather, they reject any serious use of philosophy, condemn efforts to defend Christian doctrines in current philosophical language, and content themselves with proclamation of the Christian message in its own familiar terms.

The strategy of religious isolationism marks a striking reversal of dominant church policy in the first centuries. According to the New Testament accounts, Paul argued the case for the Christian message against all comers wherever he went. Most of his work was among Jews and the Gentile *sebomenoi* already well instructed in the Old Testament. With all such people Paul argued from common premises drawn from the Old Testament. On the rare occasions when he worked with people who were not nurtured in Old Testament beliefs, he argued from beliefs more widely shared or from experiences common to all men.[2]

The writings of such second-century men as Justin Martyr, Clement of Alexandria, and even Tatian show that Christian leaders in that period of heroic faithfulness and astonishing

[2] See Acts 17:22-34 and Acts 14:11-17. If it be objected that the Book of Acts does not faithfully represent Paul's methods, it must be replied 1) that this is not yet established; 2) that in any event the first-century Christian who wrote the Acts—presumably Paul's companion Luke—believed in the methods described; and 3) that these reports are thoroughly in accord with Paul's own writing in Romans 1 and 2.

expansion eagerly went out to meet the pagan thinkers of the day, sought often to address them in their own language, and often made use of their own arguments. Even Tertullian, who roundly condemned pagan culture and the profession of teaching, showed himself to be much indebted to the pagan schools and sometimes used Greek philosophical categories in his own statements of faith.

L. Millar, in his highly useful book, *Christian Education in the First Four Centuries*,[3] shows how deeply and successfully the greatest Christian teachers of that formative period of Christian thought involved the best of pagan culture in Christian instruction. Millar, concluding a discussion of Clement of Alexandria, writes:

S. Clement certainly makes no secret of the fact that he believes education to be a great help to Christian living. And Clement was certainly not in a minority in this belief. Passage after passage in patristic writings supports his position. For most of the Fathers culture was good when rightly used.[4]

When Magnus questioned Jerome's liberal use of quotations from pagan literature, Millar notes:

In his reply Jerome points out that Moses and the Prophets had borrowed from the Gentiles, while Solomon had made use of Syrian philosophy. S. Paul, he remarks, quoted from Aratus, Callimachus, Epimenides and Menander, while it had been the common custom of Christian writers to make quotations from classical works. He cites some thirty-seven Christian authors who quote freely from pagan sources, and he says of them, "All these writers so frequently interweave in their books the doctrines and maxims of the philosophers that you might easily be at a loss which to admire most, their secular erudition or their knowledge of the scriptures."[5]

[3] London: The Faith Press, 1946.
[4] *Christian Education in the First Four Centuries*, p. 97. Used by permission.
[5] *Ibid.*, pp. 116-117. Used by permission.

In defense of monasticism attention is often called to the fact that monasteries were the chief depositories of the ancient classics which survived the Dark Ages and monks were the principal teachers of the ancient culture to the barbarians who overwhelmed the Empire. While conceding the justice of such claims, I would observe that the monasteries were fortunately not isolationist in their attitude toward classic pagan literature, but have been, throughout the centuries, busily combining Christian teaching with Greek philosophy in the scholastic systems. It is precisely in the sphere of their cultural involvement and not of their isolation that the monasteries have been especially fruitful.

C. Christian Vocation

1. Laymen called

Many people in the churches today suppose that ministers and missionaries are divinely called, but that lay Christians should be expected to choose their occupations from motives of self-interest—enlightened self-interest perhaps, but still far different from the obedient consecration expected of ministers.

The New Testament provides little or no support for such ideas. When ministry or priesthood in the church is mentioned, it is never to set apart a special class of Christians to be uniquely consecrated to God's work. There are various functions in the church, but all Christians are called to consecrated service.

Thus, Paul writes:

Now there are varieties of gifts, but the same Spirit; and there are varieties of service, but the same Lord; and there are varieties of working, but it is the same God who inspires them all in every one. To each is given the manifestation of the Spirit for the common good (1 Cor. 12:4-7).

As for the priesthood, I Pet. 2:9, addressed to the whole church dispersed among the nations (1:1), reads: "But you are a chosen race, a royal priesthood, a holy nation, God's own people, that you may declare the wonderful deeds of him who called you out of darkness into his marvelous light." Similarly, Rev. 5:9-10 represents Christ as having ransomed "for God" men "from every tribe and nation," to be "priests of our God."

Every Christian is under the lordship of Jesus Christ. The Christian does not submit only some part of himself, such as his hours of worship and prayer, to God. Faith is a commitment of the whole person. That includes his family life, his leisure, and, not least, his daily work.

Churchmen frequently wonder how they can make the voice of the church heard in the councils of government, of management, or of labor. Yet all the while parts of the professing church are *there* where the critical decisions of government and industry are being made. The trouble is that so few professing Christians in these places think of themselves as servants of Christ in their decisions. It is crucial that the church prepare its people to think of themselves in this way, to commit themselves to obey God's calling, and to fulfill his calling intelligently and faithfully where they are at work.

2. *Special calling of the church ministry*

If lawyers, farmers, and housewives are called of God to serve him as witnesses to his "wonderful deeds" (I Pet. 2:9), what is the distinctive calling of those whom we ordain as ministers of the church?

The ordained minister is called to be a specialist in the Christian message itself. Freed from the necessity of learning all the specialized knowledge and skill needed by a lawyer, a physician, or a manufacturer, he studies for the specialized task of communicating the message to people of many occupations. Through sacraments, preaching, and pastoral administration, he will bring people to confrontation with God and show them what such confrontation means. A very important task of the minister —a task but little accomplished thus far—is helping men and women of many callings to find the responsibilities and resources of Christian life in those callings.

No other work is of more crucial importance than these tasks of the ordained Christian ministry. Is there any other equal to it in the breadth of opportunity and demand? The whole church revolves around its ministry and no other persons within it have so much opportunity to affect the whole depth and range of its vitality. At the same time, the living church is the very soul of our society. All that is most sacred and most worthy of praise, all that is our best ground of hope for the present and the hereafter, centers in the church. What an awesome responsibility, but what a privilege, to be called to the guiding and nurture of its life!

The church properly gathers for worship, prayer, and instruction; then is scattered in the world to serve God by serving the varied needs of people in the name of Christ. Whether gathered for renewal of life or scattered to spend itself for its Lord in home or marketplace, it is the church.

D. The Christian World Mission

Paul says that God is "entrusting to us the message of reconciliation. So we are ambassadors for Christ, God making his appeal through us" (II Cor. 5:19b-20). As ambassadors we do not have the business of living in the privileges of the most congenial Christian fellowship we can find. An ambassador goes into foreign territory to represent his sovereign government. So all Christians are commanded to go out into the world to represent God and his divine government. They are not to expect the world to be congenial and comfortable for Christian living. For the most part it is alien territory where the genuine Christian witness will seem remote from customary ways of life and often altogether unwelcome.

1. *At home and abroad*

Many Christians live out their lives in the regions where they were born. For the great majority this will mean living in a so-called Christian country where most people pay at least lip service to Christianity and where "Christian" is a term of praise. Some, however, will answer the call of the church to work far from home, often in openly hostile territory or at least where Christians are viewed as strangers and objects of distrust. Some will go to distant lands as representatives of business or educational research. For whatever cause they are abroad, as Christians they are called to be "ambassadors for Christ." Like the people whom we call missionaries they have responsibility of bearing testimony for Christ where his name may be unknown or scarcely known.

However, whether at home or abroad, the Christian must expect to find himself in alien country. When he is at home, he will be especially tempted to conform to surrounding customs. Because the culture is familiar and nominally Christian, he may assume that it will not lead him far astray. This is a deadly temptation. There is no country in the world where prevailing customs are in obedience to Christ. Every land is alien territory. There is no country where the Christian ambassadorial mission of reconciliation is not sorely needed. Every land is a mission field.

On the other hand, this way may not be used as an excuse for refusing to engage in foreign missions. We have no right to keep all the work of the church at home on the ground that sin and need are great here as well as abroad. God cares for all his children. The church cannot be faithful to her Lord without sharing in the Lord's worldwide concern and love. The church has one mission, the world Christian mission, and all Christians are bound by their faith to share in its labor and cost.

2. *Personal and communal*

The Christian mission must be carried on personally by every Christian. Each one is called on to be an ambassador of Christ and no one else can perform his task for him. His work must be done wherever he is and in the midst of his daily occupation.

At the same time, much which must be done by the church as a whole can be made possible by the support of its various members. The conduct of worship and preaching, organized programs of Christian education, the work of hospitals and social settlements, organized evangelistic visitation, supervision of the churches, theological education of the church ministry, and the training, sending, and supporting of missions abroad and in unchurched areas at home—these are some forms of the church's corporate mission in the world.

The church's corporate mission and the personal mission of its scattered members constitute one great task in response to God's call. The two aspects are mutually supporting. The corporate church trains, spiritually strengthens, and sends forth its members for their personal work. The individual members, by their personal witness, give relevance and integrity to the corporate church and, indeed, contribute the support which makes possible its existence.

3. Denominational and ecumenical

Most church work is done through denominational organizations. The ecumenical bodies, while growing in strength, receive marginal financing from the denominations, together with supplementary contributions from individuals and foundations. Their budgets and staffs are very small as compared with those of the larger denominations. Moreover, with the exception of private financial contributions, individuals are related to the ecumenical bodies only through the member churches. Hence, to participate fully in the world Christian mission, a Christian must be actively related to an organized church.

However, the various councils of churches are increasingly important in the world Christian mission. Some things which cannot be done by single churches can be done by councils of churches. There are other tasks which can be performed better by the councils than by individual churches.

Much strategic planning for all the member churches has been done jointly in the International Missionary Council and the various commissions of the World Council of Churches. Since the union of the I.M.C. and the World Council at New Delhi in 1961, even more of such planning is being done. In the field of Christian education in the United States, much study and planning of curriculum has been done in the Division of Christian Education, National Council of Churches. This work has given rise to further, more detailed joint planning in a curriculum committee representing a number of participating churches. Similarly, training schools for church school workers are held in many places under the auspices of local and state councils.

When the churches wish to speak a word of Christian concern to a nation or to the world, they can sometimes speak much more effectively through their united councils than through their separate agencies. A word which expresses the united wisdom of representatives from many churches is likely to carry more weight than a denominational voice.

In thinking of the corporate Christian mission, we should be aware of the important complementary roles played by the churches and the councils of churches. The work is one. The churches and the councils reinforce and strengthen each other. The councils would not exist without the churches, while the churches would not be able to act so unitedly and effectively without the councils.

4. *Individual and social*

We Christians are called to be "ambassadors for Christ, God making his appeal through us" (II Cor. 5:20). Everywhere and in all relations, our warning and invitation to men is this: "We beseech you on behalf of Christ, be reconciled to God" (II Cor. 5:21).

For an individual, reconciliation means to repent of sin, to commit oneself to Christ as Savior and Lord, and to seek most faithfully to serve him thereafter in all relationships. Many relationships of individuals are structured in institutions such as government, economic order, and family life. To serve God fully in our institutions is to change the very purpose and form of the institutions in conformity to God's will. Hence our task is not only to reconcile individuals to God and to each other, but also to reconcile human institutions to the purpose of God.

To families, we must be saying, "It is not enough for a family to be prosperous and secure, healthy and happy, close-knit and loyal. It is more important to be good than to be prosperous, to be faithful to God than to be secure, to be spending yourselves for the common good than to be healthy and happy, to be loyal to God than agreeably united among yourselves. Indeed, the highest security, health, happiness, and loyalty can be found only by families which continually acknowledge church and community and God above family."

To government, Christians must be speaking with an urgent and prophetic voice today. In the name of Christ we must be declaring, "You cannot find security in hydrogen bombs or cunning alliances with oppressors of the poor. Your armaments and your alliances will bring you down to destruction unless you learn that the first requirement of a government is to be just. For a government to be just is to be useful to all its people and in all its dealings with other governments to seek first the well-being of mankind. A national government which seeks to usurp the place of God by imposing its own solutions of all world problems through violence or threat of violence will destroy itself and wreak world havoc. Turn from your proud ways and be reconciled to God who is the God of peace."

To the principalities and powers of industry, commerce, agriculture, and labor, also, we have a message from God: "Wealth and economic power were made to serve men, not men to serve wealth and power. The first business of every business is to serve people. The earning of a sound margin of profit for modernization of equipment and a reasonable extension of operation is justified only for the sake of human values. Let no man live for the sake of a living; let men earn a living in order to have life."

Loring W. Powell, a keen young businessman, with high executive responsibilities, wrote recently concerning business decisions:

There is . . . a need to weigh what is the effect now on inter-personal relationship of a given action as opposed to what its long range effect will be on such relationships. That is, we must weigh immediate goals as against ultimate goals. For the long pull, . . . the doctrine of love says that the action we take must be for the ultimate good of persons rather than things.

In any event, the businessman who is attempting to apply Christian values to his decisions will at least stop to ask, "How does this action I am about to take affect the relationship I enjoy with you? Does it improve it or destroy it?" [6]

Moreover, Powell points out, there is another relation which every Christian in the midst of economic decision must take into account. There is

another personal relationship which you enjoy; that is, your relationship with God as a person. So a similar question would be, "How does this action of mine relate with my relationship to God?" [7]

Powell stresses that religion is not to be considered "a tool for business profit." Rather, he continues,

I see in business something deeper than the making of profit. . . . I see in it an organization through which human beings seek to express their being in meaningful activity.

Within such a framework business can sit in the classroom of religion. The use of criteria of a religious nature in business action will then give the manager the ability to furnish a meaningful purpose to the efforts of himself and his people.[8]

Such messages are to be proclaimed, not only by the gathered, corporate church and by its clergy, but also by the scattered

[6] Loring W. Powell, Director, Group Annuity Sales and Service Division, John Hancock Mutual Life Insurance Company, "Foundation for Decision," a paper prepared and presented for Program for Senior Executives, Massachusetts Institute of Technology, May 5, 1961, pp. 27-28.

[7] Ibid., p. 28.

[8] Ibid., p. 29.

church through its laymen (like Mr. Powell) in all their varied occupations. They must be proclaimed both by word and by action wherever God gives the opportunity. This work in all its forms, including political, economic, and other Christian social action, is an essential part of the Christian world mission.

XI

The Centrality of Christian Education

A FEW YEARS AGO I WAS INVITED TO CONSULT WITH A PLANNING committee of a small theological seminary about their course of study. Among other matters which I thought important to emphasize, I stressed the need for a vigorous department of religious education. Thereupon one member of the committee said, "Oh, can we not take care of that by three or four evening lectures on Sunday-school work?"

Too many people in the churches have thought of religious education as only another name for Sunday school. Often they have then supposed that Sunday-school work could be done without special training by almost anyone—and to prove it pointed to some people who *were* doing it!

To all such people, and many others, religious education is one small, marginal segment of the church's work. The most successful and able people, it is thought, should be invited to supposedly more important work, such as handling the church's finances.

Being a person who is not a specialized professional in religious education, as such, I want to speak very directly and emphatically concerning the centrality of Christian education to all that the church is and does.

A. Christian Education in Church History

1. *Jesus as teacher*

The church was preceded by religious education. The Jewish leaders were—and are—called rabbis, that is, teachers, and Jesus was reared in Judaism. The effectiveness and thoroughness of the instruction he received in his youth is shown by the wealth of his citations from the Psalms and the prophets and by the depth of his own faith from the beginning of his ministry.

Jesus was himself a healer, prophet, and reformer. But in all his activities, as reported to us in the Gospels, he was above all a teacher. Everywhere and at all times, he was explaining what God requires and what are his judgments and his mercies. He welcomed questions and often answered in a way which provoked further thinking, more questions, and personal involvement.

Skilled teacher that he was, he knew that communication in real depth must usually be two-way communication. Hence much of his teaching took the form of conversation and discussion. Although the gospel writers were concerned only with recording what *he* said and did and suffered, it is impressive that his teaching was in such intimate involvement with others that his words could not be intelligently reported without including the words of others too.

2. *In the primitive church*

As soon as the church was born at Pentecost, its members, we are told, "devoted themselves to the apostles' teaching and fellowship, to the breaking of bread and the prayers" (Acts 2:42).

Like Jesus, the apostles are described as healers, but above this as teachers. The substance of the message had changed; for besides the knowledge and wisdom of Israel's historic religion, they had now, above all, to tell the good news that the nation's hope of the ages had been strangely and wonderfully fulfilled in Jesus.

Paul's letters, though they were written to deal with all kinds of practical urgent situations, are so full of careful instruction that they must be placed alongside the Gospels as among the most authoritative sources for Christian teaching.

3. *In the classical formulations of orthodoxy*

As the ancient Christians strove to teach their wonderful message to the whole Hellenistic world, they found it necessary to reformulate it in terms precisely communicable to people of non-Hebrew culture. This reformulation produced many dangerous heretical deviations which, if they had prevailed, might have robbed the church of all vitality and so brought it to an end. But similar efforts at reformulation gave rise also to the classical orthodox understanding of Christian doctrine.

4. *In subsequent church history*

Throughout church history, every great new outburst of spiritual power and forward movement has been preceded or accompanied by great efforts in theological reformulation for more effective communication of the faith to the culture of the time.

It is especially interesting to see the relation of religious education to the Wesleyan revival. Here there was not a major conceptual reformulation of the basic Protestant theology, so Methodism might seem an exception to our rule. But there was a remarkable new effort to communicate this theology to classes previously neglected. This effort included not only outdoor preaching at the mine pits, but the setting up of innumerable classes, the training of a veritable army of lay preachers and class leaders, and the printing of books and pamphlets by the tens of thousands. Many of John Wesley's sermons read like essays in systematic theology and nearly all contain much deliberate instruction. It is no accident that Methodists established schools and colleges wherever they went and set up the oldest publishing house still operating in the United States. From its very beginning, Methodism, nurtured in Wesley's "Holy Club" at Oxford University, has been, among other things, an educational movement.

B. Christian Education and Worship

The genuineness of worship in the church always depends on instruction of the people. The symbolism of vestments and altar, the religious significance of many hymns, the meanings of the sacraments and other rites—all require extensive instruction for proper understanding and appreciation. The needed teaching is done in sermons, membership training classes, church school, and literature. Where it is neglected worship declines and congregations dwindle.

Often, in the history of the church, spiritual life has been renewed in small groups where study and prayer have been combined. In recent years many of the most vital adventures in prayer and worship have occurred among college youth and in connection with the educational programs among the youth of local churches.

Indeed, when Christian education is most effective it always eventuates in prayer, worship, and obedient action. At the same time, the experiences of prayer, worship and service elevate the whole process of teaching and study to a level of seriousness and content of thought quite impossible without such experiences. Relationships of faith are the heart of the subject matter and the purpose of Christian education. Only when such relationships are actively developing is effective Christian education taking place.

C. Christian Education and Church Administration

Many a pastor finds the administrative detail of the church especially irksome. Probably he went into the ministry in the expectation of devoting himself to changing the lives of people. Now he finds himself in a never-ending round of committee meetings, statistical reports, program planning, and financial campaigns. He battles continually with a crowded calendar in the effort to find more time for the educational, pastoral, evangelistic, and prophetic ministry which he thought he had chosen to enter.

Here and there, effective pastors are finding a major solution to this problem. Their answer is to make administrative work itself a God-given opportunity for Christian education. The program may begin with a series of sermons on the real meaning and purpose of the church. Basic to all the rest is a long meeting or series of meetings in which the pastor leads the official board, vestry, or other governing body or executive committee of the church in joint study of the proper and actual purpose of their local church. Planning then takes place in relation to the purposes and priorities established in that study. The constant return to the central objectives of the church, in the planning of the various committees, gradually educates the entire church in the meaning and purpose of the church and of the Christian life itself. As the pastor draws upon the Bible and church history for the enrichment of understanding, in such settings, the educational process is especially effective because so directly related to the concrete planning and execution of the church program.

In such a setting, money raising becomes no mere struggle to meet bills and quotas, but primarily training in understanding and practicing Christian gratitude and stewardship. The appointing of a new committee is opportunity for training new people in the shared purpose of the Christian church. The planning of new church furnishings or buildings becomes a marvelous occasion for joint study of historic Christian symbolism and contemporary creative expressions of faith.

As increasing numbers of people come to share the vision of the church's real purpose, circles of responsible participation and leadership in the work widen. The minister's hands are progressively freed from administrative detail, as he increasingly devotes his attention to infusing the whole program and life of the church with authentic Christian meaning.

D. Christian Education and Missions

A large proportion of missions *is* Christian education. In long-established centers of Christian influence much Christian instruction takes place without deliberate church programming. In the home, little children are taught to say their prayers; in homes, bookshops, and public libraries are many books which frequently quote from the Bible or allude to it; in schools, even with much effort to separate public instruction from all religious concerns, Christian teachers, history of countries where faith has sometimes played a conspicuous role, and literature permeated with Christian ideas add to the total of Christian knowledge. Such holidays as Christmas and Easter, even with all their vulgar commercialization, make widely known some of the events which are celebrated by Christians everywhere. Occasionally, even television, radio, and the movies present themes from the Bible or church history, though usually with serious distortion.

When the church seeks to extend its life into new areas of the world, all this varied cultural background is sorely missed. The missionary cannot even take for granted an understanding that the Christian is expected to lead an upright and generous life. Everything that is to be known about the Christian faith must be painstakingly taught. Even churches which give little attention to teaching at home usually accept the necessity of developing ambitious educational programs in foreign fields. In sub-Sahara Africa most day schools have been started and directed by church missions and in all these schools considerable attention is given to religious education. In addition to these schools there are innumerable Sunday schools, theological schools, leadership training institutes, and membership classes, the latter very much more extended and intensive than most of their counterparts in the United States and Europe.

While missions consist, in no small part, of religious education, they depend also on Christian education for promotion and preparation in the sending churches. If people are to give the large sums of money required for missionary work, they must be taught the task and accomplishments of missions. Such instruction is accomplished in American churches by special lessons in church schools, missionary sermons, occasional visits and frequent letters from missionaries, women's study classes, leaflets, articles in church papers, books, and missionary periodicals. Moreover, the kind of motivation which induces people to contribute money or life to Christian missions requires intensive religious instruction. When, to all this, one adds the special post-college education required by most of the

larger churches in preparation of missionaries, it is seen that
the dependence of missions on Christian education is very
impressive indeed.

E. Christian Education and Social Reform

A striking characteristic of church life since World War II
has been the increasing breadth of Christian concern with social
issues. On most matters solutions have not seemed so simple
and obvious as they seemed to some in the earlier years of the
"social gospel" in the late nineteenth century. Recently the
churches' social conscience has been expressed with less passion
but with more thoughtful study. Some of the most important
utterances have come out of the World Council and National
Council of Churches. Participants have included representatives
from some churches which had been traditionally opposed to
churchly participation in discussion of political, economic, and
other social problems.

In this atmosphere many Americans, particularly, have concluded that the best method of social reform would be, not
political action, lawsuits, nor public demonstrations, but rather
the slow, sure methods of education.

Any such conclusion would certainly be a mistake. Law
establishes the limits within which some social changes can take
place. Often law determines the control of education itself.
Moreover political campaigns, lawsuits, and public demonstrations are sometimes useful means of education. Even if we rely
heavily on education, when an enlightened public opinion
favors the removal of discriminatory or other unjust laws, it
would be folly not to remove them.

Nevertheless, if we speak of Christian education in an inclusive sense, and if we are not asked to forego the action to
which enlightenment properly leads, then we may properly acknowledge that religious education must be the primary reliance
of the church for assistance to needed social reform.

Social problems are usually complex. Even when they are
not intrinsically so, deep-set prejudices prevent simple solu-

tions. The removal of prejudice requires sustained, two-way communication, information to displace misinformation, and new experience to change familiar and comfortable habits of thought and response. Such communication, information, and experience, when directed by Christian concerns is Christian education.

It is sometimes said that the whole task of the church is to convert people to Christ. Once most people are converted Christians, it is then believed, social problems will fade away.

If the task of converting to Christ is conceived in sufficient depth and inclusiveness this may be true. However, people who speak in such terms usually have in mind only the response to the kind of individualistic invitation commonly made in mass revivals, with much appeal to emotion and a minimum of instruction. People who respond to the image of "God" and "Christ" they see portrayed in such circumstances usually have only the most limited conception of what Christian living will mean. Unless they become involved later in careful and searching study, their responses to the social problems of race relations, economic strife, juvenile delinquency, Communism, and the threat of international nuclear war are likely to be much the same as those of their unconverted neighbors. They may even be worse because they may have been led to suppose that all problems may be solved as simply as the personal crises resolved in their conversion. There may result the effort to destroy all disturbers of their social ease by police or military force. Of such angry, self-righteous people some of the most fanatical rightist groups are composed.

In local churches, in whole denominations, in the various inter-church agencies, and in dealings with the public, the task of the church in social reform is largely the task of enlightening religious education.

F. Christian Education and Evangelism

Often the enthusiasts of both religious education and evangelism have supposed that the two were opposed or, at the least,

competitors for the attention and time of the church. It is easy
to understand such attitudes. *Some* evangelists have been all for
the simple emotional appeal and looked upon serious educational effort of the church as a digression from the church's main
task. *Some* religious educators have responded in kind. Thinking of evangelism in the stereotype of an ignorant rabble rouser,
they have asserted the opposition of religious education to evangelism.

However understandable, such opposition and estrangement
between the two can only be tragic for the church and for all the
people the church should serve.

Even the evangelist's most simple emotional appeal falls on
deaf ears unless there has been enough instruction of his hearers
so that such words as "God," "Christ," "sin," "the cross,"
"heaven," and "repent" have meaning and good or evil suggestive force for them. If he thinks not, let the evangelist try ad-
dressing his appeal to people who have never heard of Christ
or people to whom the word "Christ" is only a term of profanity
or the symbol of a hated alien culture. Christian education must
precede the commitment of personal faith in Christ. The more
adequate that instruction, the more meaningful the commitment
can be.

It has been widely observed also that conversions are not
usually permanent unless promptly followed by careful instruction. In any event, such instruction, by some means, is necessary if there is to be growth in Christian living.

While evangelism needs Christian education, Christian education is a failure if it does not include evangelistic pressing for
commitment of faith in Christ. The purpose of Christian education is the nurture of faith as whole commitment of the person
to Christ and of other relations rightly implied by such faith.
This purpose is evangelistic in its very nature.

Religious education has, in addition, the responsibility of
training the youth and adults of the church for the work of
witnessing to Christ. Every Christian by his dedication to Christ
is also an ambassador of God inviting others, by word and deed,

to accept the lordship of Christ over their lives. Such personal evangelistic witness requires integrity of real consecration to Christ, without self-righteous pride, but with genuine love both for God and for people. It also requires understanding and skill if it is to be effective. The nurturing of the needed consecration, humility, love, understanding, and skill is within the task of religious education.

Evangelism and Christian education are inseparable. For evangelism without education would be meaningless, while education without the invitation to faith in Christ could not be Christian.

On the other hand, faith-centered Christian education is evangelistic from its innermost purpose to its farthest outreach in the world. It begins anew whenever a Christian shares his faith in God with another person. Its work is not finished until "the kingdom of the world has become the kingdom of our Lord and of his Christ, and he shall reign for ever and ever" (Rev. 11:15).

Suggested Further Reading

On Understanding the Christian Message

Anderson, Bernhard. *Understanding the Old Testament.* Englewood Cliffs, N. J.: Prentice-Hall, Inc., 1957.

Buttrick, George A. *So We Believe, So We Pray.* Nashville: Abingdon Press, 1962.

Cave, Sydney. *The Christian Way.* New York: Philosophical Library, Inc., 1949.

DeWolf, L. Harold. *The Enduring Message of the Bible.* New York: Harper & Row, Publishers, 1960.

_____. *Present Trends in Christian Thought.* (A Reflection Book.) New York: Association Press, 1960.

_____. *A Theology of the Living Church.* Rev. ed. New York: Harper & Row, Publishers, 1960.

Harkness, Georgia. *Christian Ethics.* Nashville: Abingdon Press, 1957.

_____. *The Church and Its Laity.* Nashville: Abingdon Press, 1962.

_____. *Understanding the Christian Faith.* Nashville: Abingdon Press, 1947.

Hessert, Paul. *Introduction to Christianity.* Englewood Cliffs, N. J.: Prentice-Hall, Inc., 1958.

Hordern, William. *A Layman's Guide to Protestant Theology.* New York: The Macmillan Company, 1955.

Horton, Walter M. *Our Christian Faith.* Rev. ed. Boston: The Pilgrim Press, 1947.

Kee, Howard C. and Young, Franklin W. *Understanding the New Testament.* Englewood Cliffs, N. J.: Prentice-Hall, Inc., 1957.

Kraemer, Hendrik. *A Theology of the Laity.* Philadelphia: The Westminster Press, 1958.

Williams, Daniel D. *What Present-Day Theologians Are Thinking.* Rev. ed. New York: Harper & Row, Publishers, 1959.

On Christian Education

Bower, William C. *Christ and Christian Education.* New York and Nashville: Abingdon-Cokesbury Press, 1943.

182 TEACHING OUR FAITH IN GOD

Bowman, Clarice M. *Resources for Worship*. New York: Association Press, 1961.

————. *Ways Youth Learn*. New York: Harper & Row, Publishers, 1952.

Cully, Iris V. *The Dynamics of Christian Education*. Philadelphia: The Westminster Press, 1958.

Forsyth, Nathaniel F. *The Minister and Christian Nurture*. Nashville: Abingdon Press, 1957.

Ligon, Ernest M. *Dimensions of Character*. New York: The Macmillan Company, 1956.

Lindhorst, Frank A. *The Minister Teaches Religion*. Nashville: Abingdon Press, 1945.

Maynard, Donald M. *Your Home Can Be Christian*. Nashville: Abingdon Press, 1952.

Millar, L. *Christian Education in the First Four Centuries*. London: The Faith Press, 1946.

Miller, Randolph C. *Biblical Theology and Christian Education*. New York: Charles Scribner's Sons, 1956.

————. *Christian Nurture and the Church*. New York: Charles Scribner's Sons, 1961.

Raines, Robert A. *New Life in the Church*. New York: Harper & Row, Publishers, 1961.

Sherrill, Lewis J. *The Rise of Christian Education*. New York: The Macmillan Company, 1950.

Sloyan, Gerard S., editor. *Shaping the Christian Message: Essays in Religious Education*. New York: The Macmillan Company, 1958.

Vieth, Paul H. *The Church and Christian Education*. St. Louis: Bethany Press, 1947.

————. *The Church School*. Philadelphia: United Church Press, 1957.

Wyckoff, D. Campbell. *The Gospel and Christian Education*. Philadelphia: The Westminster Press, 1959.

————. *The Theory and Design of Christian Education Curriculum*. Philadelphia: The Westminster Press, 1961.

Index

183